REBOOT

with Kayla

A 4-week toolkit for rediscovering your best self

REBOOT

with Kayla

KAYLA ITSINES

In loving memory of Deb (@fitwithsweat), a beloved member of the Sweat Community, who showed us what it truly means to be a strong woman.

CONTENTS

INTRODUCTION

Welcome to *Reboot with Kayla*! I'm Kayla Itsines, co-founder and head trainer at Sweat. And I'd love for you to think of me as your coach too! I'm here to cheer you on over the next four weeks and can't wait for you to discover workouts that meet you where you are, meals you'll love and practical tools to help set you up for long-term success.

I've been helping women achieve their health and fitness goals since 2009 and have trained my clients everywhere from in gyms and parks to my parents' backyard and even in packed-out stadiums.

The fitness landscape was so different back when I started out working as a personal trainer and it needed to change. The weights section of most gyms felt masculine, intimidating and, to be honest, pretty unwelcoming to women.

Looking around, all I saw being provided to women was men's programming, with minor or no adjustments for women's bodies. That seemed crazy to me. I just felt like there was no consideration for women's bodies and needs when it came to these gym plans, such as our menstrual cycles, hormones, pregnancy and conditions such as endometriosis. If you've ever tried to join your toddler jumping on a trampoline after giving birth, you'll know that men's fitness programs just don't cut it for women.

And yet, for some reason, people still often talk down about certain movements by calling them 'girly' exercises. I wanted to create a space where there was no such thing as 'girly push-ups' or 'women's weights'. A place where the female fitness experience wasn't just accommodated, but championed.

That's why Sweat isn't just another fitness app, program or quick fix. It's a community. A collective of women from all over the world who are determined to grow stronger together in body and mind. Women who are brand new to fitness, women who are hitting reboot after a break and women who are already smashing their goals.

And no matter what age they are, what life stage they're in and what fitness level they're at, they all have each other's backs. And they have since day one.

If you don't know me from the Sweat app, chances are you might know me from a PDF. Back when I was training women one-on-one, I started sharing their stories on Instagram. More and more women began reaching out to me, asking for me to share my workouts so they could train just like my clients were, so we decided to sell my 12-week training guide as a PDF. To be honest, when we first released it, I thought no one would buy it. I was wrong. It went *crazy*. But here's the thing about those original BBG guides. You could buy one copy and send it to your friend, your sister, your mum, your neighbour's boyfriend's cousin's best friend – whoever. Suddenly, it was everywhere.

Social media helped my programs reach an audience that would have been unimaginable at the start of my career. But even back in those early days, *long* before the BBG PDF went viral or the Sweat app was launched, I'd realised what women were really looking for was connection, community and empowerment. I truly believe my success has never just been about me. It's been about the women I train and the relationships they've built - with me, with the Sweat Community, and most importantly, with themselves.

Friendships were built across borders and hashtags, group chats became a place to celebrate *and* vent (turns out not everyone loves burpees as much as I do), and women around the world discovered they were stronger, together. Some of these women even went on to become Sweat trainers themselves or pursue careers in health and fitness.

After launching the guide we had so many requests for the programs to be on an app, and Sweat with Kayla – the original app – was born. Today, the Sweat app is home to over 50 programs and more than 13,000 workouts designed by women, for women, offering the support of a global community and backed by years of science, experience, results and a whole lot of Sweat.

On the Sweat app, you can try everything from a high-intensity session with me, to Pilates or barre, or finish your day with a relaxing yoga flow. You'll also find plenty of recipes, our incredible forum and the latest health and wellbeing advice. All you have to do is show up and Sweat – we've got the rest.

The Sweat Community is my *why* when it comes to fitness. It's helped women all over the world get confident and comfortable with fitness *and* in themselves. Our purpose is to empower women through fitness, because I know firsthand how movement can change your life. And if you're reading this, you might be ready to make a change yourself.

Perhaps your fitness routine has taken a back seat for too long. Maybe you're coming back to exercise after an unexpected setback. You might just be looking for a way to reset your goals and reignite your love for movement after an extended holiday. Or maybe you've been inspired by a new year, month or week to focus on your health. This book is for *any* woman who wants to recommit to her goals and put herself first.

Recently, I had to reboot my own fitness journey after welcoming my second child, Jax. But my experience returning to fitness after Jax's birth was *so* different from the first time around.

After Arna's birth in 2019, for the first time in my life, I felt completely lost when it came to moving my body and planning my routine. I felt connected to every woman who had ever felt intimidated walking into a gym and every woman who had been completely overwhelmed at the start of a workout. Despite being a personal trainer, I really struggled in that first session, six weeks after welcoming a beautiful baby girl into the world.

I struggled, because no matter what I did, everything hurt, and I had no idea when it was going to get better. It felt like my body had been taken from me. And yes, there were tears. How I felt during that season of my life was a huge motivator for me to release my post-pregnancy program in 2019, followed by my low-impact program. The feedback from those programs and the requests from our community then led me to release my pregnancy program in 2022. I'm so proud that Sweat now has training options for women at every stage of life.

Returning to fitness after becoming a mum is one of the hardest things I've ever done. And no matter where you are in your own health and fitness journey today, I want you to know: it's okay to feel a little overwhelmed. Focus on what you *can* do rather than what you can't do. Make modifications. But make a commitment to yourself and remind yourself that you *can* do hard things. I'll be alongside you every step of the way.

Remember, fitness is about so much more than a number on a scale. It's setting a new goal and hitting it. It's discovering the endurance to dance for hours with your friends. It's trying a new training style. It's about feeling confident in the gym. It's about progress, not perfection. And it's about realising you're capable of SO MUCH MORE than you first thought was possible.

We all have to start somewhere. So let's hit reboot together.

MY WELLBEING PHILOSOPHY

My family and community are what's most important to me. So many things have changed and affected the way I see health and fitness over the years, but my amazing family and the incredible Sweat Community have played the biggest roles in all of this. No one has informed my approach to fitness and wellbeing more, and that's why giving people that same sense of connection means so much to me.

I was really lucky to grow up in a family where food was something to be celebrated and movement was just a part of everyday life. Seeing a healthy and balanced lifestyle role modelled for me, day in and day out by those around me, meant I never saw exercise as punishment or food as something to be denied. It's only as I've gotten older that I've realised just how much of a gift this was to my younger self – I know that for so many women in my community, this just wasn't the case.

Growing up, my mum never put herself down or talked negatively about her body around my sister Leah and me. I never saw my mum or my yiayia comparing themselves to others or refusing to eat certain foods. And exercise was never something we *had* to do – it was something we *got* to do.

I've always taken so much joy out of being able to move my body, whether it's playing sports or going for a morning walk. But my attitude towards fitness *and* my body has changed since becoming a mum. Motherhood has made me more understanding and patient, and has given me a whole new appreciation for my body. I am so grateful for everything my body is capable of, whether that's pull-ups or carrying my children. My body was Arna and Jax's first home – how could I not be in awe of it?!

As a mother, I want to pass this mindset on to my own children. I want them to be confident in their bodies – not just in how they look, but proud of what their bodies are capable of. After all, we only get one body. We should treat it with the love and respect it deserves every single day.

I also want to make sure Arna and Jax know that food is something to be enjoyed with family and friends and a way to nourish their bodies. That's why there are no 'good' or 'bad' foods in our house. Just as my parents showed me, I want Arna and Jax to not only see me achieving my fitness goals and enjoying plenty of nutritious food, but also know I'm not afraid to eat a doughnut, either.

Ultimately, my fitness and wellbeing philosophy can be distilled into three words: keep it simple.

Since the beginning of my career, I have tried to make fitness as simple and accessible as possible so that any woman feels empowered to start. No matter what kind of time, space or equipment you have available, I want to help you not only to move your body, but to *enjoy* it. I want to help you develop a powerful and positive relationship with yourself and focus on your mindset just as much as your movement.

As your trainer, I want to encourage you to take a sustainable approach to fuelling your body, which includes eating the foods you love. I don't diet, calorie count or say no to certain foods, which is why the recipes we've included in this book are only there to nourish you. Yes, food is fuel, but it's also fun and it should feel good.

When setting your health and fitness goals, make sure they won't get in the way of your life. You want your goals to help you lead a healthy, balanced lifestyle you can enjoy. I don't want you to ever feel like you need to say no to dinner with your friends because you're worried about calories, need to rearrange your whole schedule to make time for a lengthy workout, or find you're completely depleted from overtraining. Your health and fitness routine should always *add* to your life, not take away from it.

My fitness programs (including the one you'll find in this book!) have been designed to help you train effectively and efficiently, no matter how much time you have. I want you to be able to work out two to three times a week and achieve your fitness goals. This training philosophy is the foundation of *all* my programs.

I truly believe that something is always better than nothing when it comes to fitness, and this is something that really rings true for me at this time of my life. I have two small kids and a really busy job. Sometimes, I'm just *tired*. On those days when I'm just not feeling it, I opt for something small instead. Perhaps it's some light stretches after putting the kids to bed for the night or even a walk with the family. Make bite-sized exercise snacks part of your everyday routine, and soon you'll find that staying active is just second nature.

When you're training with me, I want you to know that I practise what I preach. I'm not going to sit here and tell you to do one thing, but then go and do something else myself. I absolutely follow my own advice, which is why what I recommend for you as your trainer – such as walking, making time for rest and not denying yourself the foods that you love – are things I fundamentally believe in. I also think it's important for me to stay in my lane. I'm a personal trainer, not a physiotherapist, dietitian or doctor. I wholeheartedly believe I should only use my platform to give advice when I am qualified to do so. That's why I've collaborated with experts to develop the recipes you'll find in this book. If and when you need professional advice, seek it out. For example, I might be a personal trainer, but I worked with a women's health physiotherapist after my C-sections and found their support to be invaluable.

People talk a lot about listening to your body, but one of the most important things I think you can do in life (not just in fitness) is to learn the difference between what you want and need. Sometimes your body does genuinely *need* rest, but sometimes you just *want* to chill out when you could easily give 110 per cent in a workout. Without knowing the difference and challenging yourself sometimes, 'listening to your body' can become an excuse for never taking action towards your goals.

When you do need to take a break or to slow down, don't doubt yourself – you *can* do anything you put your mind to, if you work hard and put the time in. It's all about being patient and remembering why this is important to you. I had *so* many people tell me I would never be able to skip again after having kids. Actually, I had a lot of people tell me I wouldn't be able to do a lot of things. After slowly and gradually building my fitness back up after Jax's birth, I'm happy to say I *can* still skip after two kids.

Never forget just how incredible you and your body are. I can't wait to see what you can do.

HOW TO USE THIS BOOK

Reboot with Kayla is more than just a workout plan or a journal. It's a toolkit for success. Because the Sweat team and I know what you do when you're *not* exercising is just as important as your training time, we've designed this book to help reignite your love for movement, wellbeing and exercise.

We'll take you through four weeks of workouts that meet you where you are, give you some nourishing meal ideas and offer prompted journalling to help you check in and reflect along the way. We'll hit the reboot button on your fitness journey together and tune in to your why, to set you on the path to feeling amazing in yourself. The best part? This story doesn't end when the book does. This is something you can come back to time and time again when you feel like a reset.

FOUR WEEKS – AND BEYOND

Over the next four weeks, we want to help you feel your best – inside *and* out. How? By arming you with the tools you need to make fitness a habit. It may be tempting to skip straight to the last section or dial up the intensity of your training on day one, but we can all benefit from building a solid foundation right from the start. Each week has a focus:

Week 1: Mindset. This week is all about finding a positive headspace and getting moving in small but impactful ways. Let's start this journey feeling empowered to hit the ground running.

Week 2: Movement. Now you've nailed the fundamentals, let's progress with a strength circuit *and* an extra workout session per week. This week, we'll focus on building intention and routine.

Week 3: Motivation. This is when the program ramps up, with a more challenging circuit workout. Mentally, this is also when things can start to feel difficult, so let's help you push through the self-doubt and get it done!

Week 4: Momentum. You've put in so much hard work to get to this point, and we want to build on everything we've learned so far to make fitness not just part of your routine, but something you *love*. How do we keep the momentum up? We'll do it together.

Each week we'll also dive a little deeper into key topics to help you unlock even more impact from your reboot journey. Think of these as thought starters and extra fire to help keep your fitness spark alight.

WEEK 1 KEY: **GRATITUDE**

WEEK 2 KEY: **WALKING**

WEEK 3 KEY: **COMMUNITY**

WEEK 4 KEY: **FUEL**

EXERCISES

The Sweat team and I have created a workout program tailored to each of these four stages. Each week, you'll see a list of sessions to choose from – a mix of walking, mobility and strength workouts – complete with a specified number of sessions for the week. If you're coming back from an injury or setback, or simply want to take a gentler approach at first, you could opt for two walks instead of the circuit workouts.

Each exercise has a series of illustrated steps, so you can see how they're done. Getting your form right is *so* important, so we've also included some tips to make sure you not only perform these exercises correctly, but also get the most out of them – you'll find those on pages 78–79.

When it comes to the workouts, it's not about being the strongest or the fastest, especially in the beginning. That's why don't focus on time limits for the exercises and instead generally note the number of reps to aim for. Just show up for yourself and do your best to complete the workout.

RECIPES

If you've followed me for a while, you'll know I feel pretty strongly about embracing a healthy, balanced diet. I'm lucky to have some amazing cooks in my family, and for us, enjoying a meal is one of our favourite ways to spend time together. The Sweat team and I have hand-picked some delicious meals to form part of your reboot journey, and I *promise* they don't require too much prep or hours spent in the kitchen. Remember, this isn't a diet book. I'm not into restrictive eating, or 'good' or 'bad' labels for food. Instead, you'll find nutrient-rich recipes for breakfast, lunch, dinner and snacks, all designed to keep your energy up.

The included recipes are a guide, not a strict plan. We know that between work, family, study and whatever else you have on your plate, deciding what's for dinner at the end of the day can sometimes be a bit of a nightmare. These easy ideas are here to take the guesswork out of choosing filling, nourishing meals you'll actually enjoy. And there are plenty of options for any dietary requirements you might have, too!

JOURNAL PAGES AND PEP TALKS

If the past few years have taught us anything, life can feel pretty overwhelming at times. In this book, we want to help you eat well and make exercise a habit. But one of my favourite things about exercise is how it makes me feel – something I want everyone to discover for themselves. That's why I want you to take the time to think about how you're feeling in body *and* mind. In each section, you'll find pep talks from me to inspire you along the way, as well as journal pages filled with prompts to reflect on where you're at so far.

If sitting down to write out your answers feels alien to you, I totally get it. One of my favourite ways to check in with myself is to go for a walk. Try that (*without* a podcast or music on) and have a go at answering the prompts in your head.

We created these journal pages as a space for you to create a visual record of your journey. Track your daily wins, hurdles, motivations and reflections, and tailor the program so it works for you and your goals. And on those days when you're just not feeling it, look back at these pages to remember why you started.

You'll also find some of my favourite quotes throughout the book. I like to keep these in mind whenever I'm having a low motivation day. Hopefully you get just as much out of them as I do.

RECIPES

REBOOT RECIPES

Let's talk about the food we use to fuel our bodies.

My experience has shown me that so many women have complicated relationships with food because we are bombarded with countless conflicting messages about what to eat, what to avoid and how big your serving sizes should be. But the Sweat team and I want you to hear the words 'healthy eating' *without* your mind jumping to diets and restriction. We want these recipes to inspire you to eat a range of different nutrients and flavours – and importantly, get the energy you need to keep active. It goes without saying, but drinking plenty of water is a must too.

My personal definition of 'healthy eating' is a balanced approach that takes both science and intuition into account. I don't diet, but I do think about the food I put into my body, because it gives me the tools I need for my body to function and perform day-to-day, physically *and* mentally.

Remember, it's important to eat a wide variety of food each day. With this in mind, we've included a range of recipes to help support you on your health and fitness journey. You'll see lots inspired by my Greek heritage (you cannot go wrong with my Tzatziki recipe on page 65!) as well as treats like my Raspberry Choc Top Overnight Oats on page 27 that make for a great pre-workout breakfast or snack. You'll find plenty of Sweat Community favourites from over the years, too!

We all lead increasingly busy lives, so we've tried to keep these recipes simple. Most will take less than an hour to prep and serve and some can be made even faster with pre-portioned proteins, or adjusted to suit a meal-prep routine.

The best meals are the ones we love and come back to time and time again, and that's our hope for the recipes in this book. Enjoy!

Breakfast Wrap

Prep time: 5 mins | **Cook time:** 10 mins | **Serves:** 1

Breakfast for me is usually something savoury, and this wrap is flavourful, filling and quick to whip together once your veggies are prepped. This is a great one for kids (Arna loves it!) or, if you're lactose-intolerant like me, leave out the cheese. If you like to spice things up you can add your favourite hot sauce, for more fibre and flavour go for wholemeal wraps, or swap out the wrap for a gluten-free option.

INGREDIENTS:

1 teaspoon olive oil
¼ medium red capsicum, finely diced
¼ red onion, finely diced
1 small handful baby spinach leaves, chopped
1 large egg, lightly beaten
30 g grated cheddar cheese
sea salt and ground black pepper
1 medium wholemeal or gluten-free wrap
¼ avocado, sliced

METHOD:

1. Add olive oil to a non-stick frying pan and heat over medium heat. Add the capsicum and red onion and cook for 5 minutes, stirring occasionally, until softened. Add the baby spinach and stir to combine, cooking until the spinach is wilted. Transfer the vegetable mixture to a small bowl and set aside.

2. Reheat the same pan over low heat. Add the egg and half the cheese and stir to combine. As the mixture begins to set, gently push the egg across the pan with a spatula to form large folds. Ensure that you push the mixture from different directions and include the mixture from around the edge of the pan. Do not stir constantly. Continue to cook until the egg is just set, then immediately remove from the heat. Season with salt and pepper to taste.

3. To serve, place the wrap on a serving plate. Top with the avocado, cooked vegetable mix, scrambled egg and the remaining cheese. Roll up to enclose the filling.

Spinach and Feta Breakfast Muffins

Prep time: 15 mins | **Cook time:** 20 mins | **Makes:** 6 muffins

Having a batch of muffins on hand can really take the stress out of busy weekday mornings. It's also a great way to use up that bag of spinach you forgot about or whatever vegetables you have left over in the fridge. If you don't have feta, feel free to use whatever cheese you do have, or add the cheese at the end if you want to make a few lactose-free.

INGREDIENTS:

olive oil spray
6 large eggs
sea salt and ground black
    pepper
30 g baby spinach leaves,
    chopped
½ small red capsicum, diced
35 g feta cheese, crumbled

METHOD:

1. Preheat oven to 180°C (160°C fan-forced) and lightly spray 6 holes of a standard 80 ml muffin tin with oil.

2. Whisk the eggs in a medium bowl and season with salt and pepper to taste.

3. Add the spinach, capsicum and feta cheese and mix gently to combine.

4. Pour the mixture into the prepared muffin holes until each one is three-quarters full.

5. Bake for 15–20 minutes, or until set and the tops are golden brown. Serve warm or at room temperature.

Tips

Muffins will keep in the fridge for up to 3 days.

Cut strips of baking paper roughly 3 cm wide x 15 cm long and place them in each muffin hole in a cross shape to help lift the muffins from the pan when cooked.

Avo Smash with Mexican Salsa

Prep time: 15 mins | **Cook time:** 5 mins | **Serves:** 1

Everyone loves avocado on toast, but this version adds a little something extra. There is absolutely no need to go for a pre-made guac, especially if you can find fresh avocados on special at the supermarket. The ingredient that brings it all together is a pinch of spice – you won't want to make your avocado on toast without it. If you don't like cumin, I often use cayenne pepper.

INGREDIENTS:

1 small tomato, diced
1 tablespoon diced red onion
1 tablespoon chopped
  coriander
1 garlic clove, crushed
pinch ground cumin
½ lime, juiced (or to taste)
sea salt and ground black
  pepper
1 slice sourdough bread or
  gluten-free bread
½ avocado, sliced

METHOD:

1. For the Mexican salsa, combine the tomato, red onion, coriander, garlic, cumin and lime juice in a small bowl. Season with salt and pepper to taste.

2. Meanwhile, toast the bread to your liking.

3. To serve, place the toast on a serving plate. Top with the avocado slices and Mexican salsa.

Greek Scrambled Eggs

Prep time: 5 mins | **Cook time:** 10 mins | **Serves:** 1

Scrambled eggs are a versatile and filling breakfast, and even better with fresh cherry tomatoes and Greek-style flavours. If you're making a big batch of scrambled eggs for a crowd, my rule of thumb is two eggs per person, depending on how hungry everyone is or what you're serving them with!

INGREDIENTS:

2 large eggs
½ teaspoon dried oregano
sea salt and ground black
    pepper
1 teaspoon olive oil
1 tablespoon diced
    brown onion
1 garlic clove, crushed
5 cherry tomatoes, halved
    or quartered
20 g feta cheese, crumbled

METHOD:

1. Whisk the eggs and oregano in a small bowl. Season with salt and pepper to taste.

2. Heat the olive oil in a medium saucepan over medium-low heat. Add the diced onion and cook for 2–3 minutes, stirring occasionally, until soft and translucent. Add the garlic and cook for another minute, stirring constantly.

3. Pour in the egg mixture. As the egg begins to set, gently push it across the pan with a wooden spoon or spatula to form large folds. Do not stir constantly. Continue to cook until no visible liquid egg remains, then immediately remove from the heat.

4. To serve, place the scrambled eggs on a plate with the cherry tomatoes. Top with crumbled feta cheese.

Tip

Keep diced onion in an airtight container in the fridge so you can easily grab as much as you need for different recipes. It will keep for up to 1 week.

Strawberry Maple French Toast

Prep time: 10 mins | **Cook time:** 10 mins | **Serves:** 1

This French toast recipe is super simple and comes together before you know it. If you have kids, this is a great one to make together too. Feel free to swap the strawberries for whatever fruit is in season and use an alternative milk or gluten-free bread if you have any dietary requirements. I use an oil spray because I find it browns the bread more evenly, and it's easy to add more if your bread starts to stick.

INGREDIENTS:

2 tablespoons milk of your choice
1 large egg, beaten
½ teaspoon ground cinnamon (plus extra to serve, optional)
½ teaspoon pure vanilla extract
olive oil spray
2 slices wholemeal bread or gluten-free bread
4 strawberries, sliced
1 tablespoon pure maple syrup

METHOD:

1. Whisk the milk, egg, cinnamon and vanilla extract together in a shallow dish.

2. Lightly spray a non-stick frying pan with oil and heat over medium heat.

3. Soak the bread in the milk mixture briefly, turning to evenly coat both sides. Let any excess mixture drip off. Cook for 4–5 minutes on each side, until lightly browned.

4. To serve, place the French toast on a serving plate. Top with the strawberries and a little more ground cinnamon, if desired. Drizzle over the maple syrup and serve.

Raspberry Choc Top Overnight Oats

Prep time: 10 mins + overnight chilling | **Serves:** 2

Who doesn't love berries and chocolate? This delicious brekky combo is something you can easily make the night before. It's so quick and straightforward and something you'll look forward to eating every single day. Like all overnight oat recipes, it's up to you if you want to switch up the fruit and seeds combo, but you can't go wrong with berries and chocolate.

INGREDIENTS:

90 g rolled oats
1 cup (250 ml) milk of
   your choice
2 tablespoons pure
   maple syrup
2 tablespoons cacao powder
1 tablespoon chia seeds
1 teaspoon pure
   vanilla extract
90 g fresh raspberries,
   roughly mashed,
   plus extra to serve
50 g dark chocolate,
   chopped
1 teaspoon coconut oil

METHOD:

1. Place the oats, milk, maple syrup, cacao powder, chia seeds, vanilla extract and raspberries in a bowl and mix until well combined.

2. Meanwhile, place the dark chocolate and coconut oil into a small bowl and heat in the microwave in 20-second bursts, stirring in between, until the chocolate is melted and smooth.

3. Transfer the oat mixture into 2 jars or bowls. Add the melted dark chocolate to each jar of oats to create a 'choc top' layer. Cover with plastic film or lids and place in the refrigerator to chill overnight.

4. Top with extra raspberries to serve.

Supergreen Protein Smoothie

Prep time: 5 mins | **Serves:** 1

Smoothies are such a delicious and easy way to kickstart your day with nutrients, and hardly any prep or time is needed! If you love peanut butter, this take on a classic green smoothie will keep you energised for hours, thanks to the protein and healthy fats. Adding some spinach is a great way to make any smoothie more vitamin-rich or get more greens into your day if you haven't had enough.

INGREDIENTS:

½ cup (125 ml) unsweetened coconut milk
(or milk of choice)
½ frozen banana
1 recommended serve protein powder
of choice (optional)
1 medjool date, pitted
1–2 tablespoons peanut butter
1 large handful baby spinach leaves
ice cubes

METHOD:

1. Simply add all of your smoothie ingredients into a high-powered blender and blend until smooth.

Blueberry Pie Smoothie

Prep time: 5 mins | **Serves:** 1

This smoothie is inspired by blueberry crumble, and the combo of vanilla protein, rolled oats, cinnamon and berries make for a brekky that feels like dessert. Batch up the frozen fruit in your freezer so all you have to do is throw the ingredients in a blender and mix!

INGREDIENTS:

1 cup (250 ml) unsweetened coconut milk
(or milk of choice)
100 g frozen blueberries
½ frozen banana
1 recommended serve protein powder
of choice (optional)
60 g rolled oats
pinch ground cinnamon
ice cubes

METHOD:

1. Simply add all of your smoothie ingredients into a high-powered blender and blend until smooth.

Easy Bean Quesadilla

Prep time: 10 mins | **Cook time:** 10 mins | **Serves:** 1

Taking the time to pull together a healthy lunch helps me to stay energised and avoid that 3 pm slump. Packed full of nutrients, veggies and flavour, quesadillas tick a lot of boxes. To make the clean-up process a breeze and get them crispy on all sides, I use a sandwich press instead of a pan, and if you've got sour cream on hand you can serve it on the side.

INGREDIENTS:

75 g tinned four-bean mix, rinsed and drained
30 g frozen corn kernels
¼ medium red capsicum, diced
½ teaspoon garlic powder
¼ teaspoon chilli powder
¼ teaspoon ground cumin
sea salt and ground black pepper
¼ avocado, mashed
1 medium tortilla wrap
30 g cheddar cheese, grated
20 g light sour cream, to serve (optional)

METHOD:

1. Preheat a sandwich press.

2. Heat a medium saucepan over medium heat. Add the four-bean mix, corn kernels, capsicum, garlic powder, chilli powder and cumin. Cook for 4–5 minutes until heated through, stirring occasionally. Season with salt and pepper to taste.

3. Spread the mashed avocado on one half of the tortilla wrap and sprinkle over half the cheese.

4. Place the open wrap on the sandwich press. Top the avocado and cheese with the bean mixture and remaining cheese, then fold the wrap in half to enclose the filling. Gently press down the sandwich press lid.

5. Toast for 3–5 minutes, until the wrap is crisp and golden brown.

6. Remove the quesadilla from the sandwich press, transfer to a serving plate and cut in half. Serve with sour cream on the side, if using.

Salmon and Rice Bowl

Prep time: 10 mins | **Cook time:** 20 mins | **Serves:** 1

A rice bowl is one of my go-to lunches and an easy way to pack in loads of nutrients. The salmon is so easy to cook, either in the oven or an air fryer, and although sushi rice adds a delicious flavour and texture, using whatever rice you have in your pantry works just as well. Kewpie mayo dressing, though, is a must.

INGREDIENTS:

1 small salmon fillet (skin off)
olive oil spray
sea salt and ground
    black pepper
70 g sushi rice
75 g shelled frozen
    edamame, thawed
1 handful leafy greens
    such as baby spinach
    or shredded kale
1 tablespoon soy sauce
    or tamari
1 tablespoon Kewpie
    mayonnaise
sesame seeds, toasted,
    to serve

METHOD:

1. Preheat oven to 180°C (160°C fan-forced) and line a baking tray with baking paper.

2. Lightly spray the salmon with oil and season on both sides with salt and pepper to taste. Transfer the salmon to the lined baking tray and bake for 12–15 minutes, until the salmon has changed colour and can be easily flaked with a fork. Alternatively, cook the salmon in an air fryer for 10–15 minutes at 170°C.

3. In the meantime, cook the sushi rice and edamame separately, according to packet instructions.

4. To serve, assemble the rice, salmon, edamame and leafy greens in a bowl. Top with soy sauce and Kewpie mayonnaise, and sprinkle with sesame seeds.

Tip
Cook salmon fillets in advance and use microwaveable rice pouches, for a grab-and-go option.

Simple Caesar Salad

Prep time: 10 mins | **Cook time:** 12 mins | **Serves:** 2

For a quick, easy and tasty salad that will fill you up, try this caesar salad. The eggs provide a great source of protein to make the salad filling, and you could easily swap the croutons for shredded chicken if you want something more substantial or you're gluten-free.

INGREDIENTS:

2 large eggs
2 slices wholemeal bread
    (optional)
90 g low-fat plain yoghurt
1 garlic clove, crushed
1 lemon, juiced (or to taste)
sea salt and ground
    black pepper
2 large handfuls cos lettuce
    leaves, chopped
10 cherry tomatoes, halved
40 g parmesan cheese,
    shaved

METHOD:

1. Place the eggs into a small saucepan and pour in enough water to cover the eggs by at least 6 cm. Bring to the boil, uncovered. Once boiling, immediately cover with a lid and remove from the heat. Allow the eggs to sit in the hot water for 10 minutes. Cool the eggs under cold running water, then peel and cut into quarters.

2. Meanwhile, toast the bread to your liking, then cut into small squares.

3. To make the dressing, whisk the yoghurt, garlic and lemon juice together in a small bowl. Season with salt and pepper to taste.

4. Place the lettuce, tomatoes and dressing in a mixing bowl and toss gently to combine.

5. To serve, place the salad into serving bowls and top with the croutons, egg and shaved parmesan.

Tips

For an even higher protein option, swap out the croutons for 100 g of cooked chicken – shredded or rotisserie chicken works perfectly.

Hard boil 3 or more eggs in advance and use them for easy protein-filled snacks.

Kayla's Go-to Tuna Salad

Prep time: 15 mins | **Serves:** 2

My community knows I eat this all the time and it only takes 15 minutes to put together. It may seem like a long list of ingredients but they're all easy to prep, and adding the roasted capsicum and basil packs in so much flavour. I've always got balsamic glaze and balsamic vinegar in my house for this. Delicious.

INGREDIENTS:

185 g tinned tuna in springwater, drained
250 g cooked brown or white rice, cooled
2 Lebanese cucumbers, chopped
12 cherry tomatoes, quartered
2 spring onions, finely sliced
¼ red onion, finely sliced
1 large handful fresh basil leaves
2 tablespoons chopped roasted capsicum or sundried tomatoes
2 tablespoons olive oil
1 tablespoon balsamic vinegar
½ teaspoon chilli flakes (optional)
sea salt and ground black pepper
balsamic glaze, to serve

METHOD:

1. Combine the tuna, rice, cucumber, cherry tomatoes, spring onion, red onion, basil and roasted capsicum in a medium bowl.

2. To make the dressing, whisk the olive oil, balsamic vinegar and chilli flakes (if using) in a small bowl or jug, and season with salt and pepper to taste.

3. Pour the dressing over the salad and toss well to combine. Serve drizzled with a little balsamic glaze.

Tip

I like to use microwaveable rice packets to save time on prep – any type of rice works well in this dish!

Cherry Tomato and Bocconcini Bruschetta

Prep time: 5 mins | **Cook time:** 5 mins | **Serves:** 1

The combination of tomatoes, fresh basil and bocconcini is one of my favourites, and throwing it all on top of a bagel is a great option for a lunch (or breakfast!). The basil garnish, plus pepper and plenty of salt, really brings out the flavour of the tomatoes.

INGREDIENTS:

1 bagel, halved
4 cherry tomatoes, sliced
4 cherry bocconcini, sliced
1–2 sprigs fresh basil,
    leaves picked
sea salt and ground
    black pepper

METHOD:

1. Toast the bagel to your liking.

2. Top with the sliced cherry tomatoes, bocconcini and fresh basil. Season with salt and pepper to taste.

Tip
Tossing the topping ingredients together with the salt and pepper a little ahead of time will make them more 'saucy'.

Falafel Wrap with Tzatziki

Prep time: 10 mins + 30 mins chilling | **Cook time:** 10 mins | **Serves:** 1

I'm so proud to be Greek and food is a huge part of our family life. If there is any chance for me to put tzatziki on something, I'll take it. I recommend using a food processor for the falafel mix, but a small blender will do if it's all you have on hand. They do take a bit of time to prep and chill, so make sure you've got enough time for that. Once they're ready, the wrap is quick and easy to assemble – don't forget the tzatziki!

INGREDIENTS:

200 g tinned chickpeas, rinsed and drained
¼ small brown onion, diced
1 garlic clove
½ teaspoon ground cumin
½ teaspoon ground coriander
2 tablespoons chopped parsley
1 tablespoon wholemeal flour
sea salt and ground black pepper
olive oil spray
1 wholemeal or gluten-free wrap
Kayla's Tzatziki, to serve (see page 65)
½ small tomato, sliced
¼ Lebanese cucumber, sliced
2–4 lettuce leaves

METHOD:

1. To make the falafel, place the chickpeas, onion, garlic, cumin, coriander, parsley and flour into a food processor. Season with salt and pepper and process until almost smooth.

2. Alternatively, for a chunkier falafel, pulse half the chickpeas in a food processer until rough like large grains, then set aside. Process the remaining ingredients with salt and pepper into a smooth paste then mix with the rougher chickpeas to bind.

3. To make 3 falafel, roll the mixture into 3 even balls, then flatten into 1 cm thick patties. Place on a plate, cover with plastic film and refrigerate for 30 minutes.

4. Spray a non-stick frying pan with oil and heat over medium heat. Add the falafel and cook for 4–5 minutes on each side, until golden brown and cooked through.

5. To serve, place the wrap on a serving plate. Spread with tzatziki and place the tomato, cucumber and lettuce leaves down the middle of the wrap. Top with the falafel and roll up to enclose.

Tip

To save time, the falafel can be made and cooked the night before. Store in an airtight container in the fridge for up to 5 days.

Prawn Noodle Stir-fry

Prep time: 15 mins | **Cook time:** 15 mins | **Serves:** 4

A noodle stir-fry makes it easy to get lots of flavour-packed vegetables into your diet. Anything goes here, but I love to include plenty of bok choy, broccoli, carrots and capsicum. If you're not a fan of prawns, swap them out for your protein of choice – try crispy tofu for a vegetarian option. One chilli is listed here for spice, but add as much or as little as you'd like.

INGREDIENTS:

⅓ cup (80 ml) soy sauce
   or tamari
¼ cup (60 ml) honey
2 tablespoons lemon juice
1 tablespoon cornflour
1 teaspoon sesame oil
20 medium raw prawns
½ head broccoli,
   cut into florets
1 carrot, sliced
1 bok choy, roughly chopped
1 red capsicum, chopped
4 garlic cloves, crushed
2 teaspoons finely grated
   fresh ginger
1 fresh red chilli,
   sliced (optional)
450 g shelf-fresh hokkien
   noodles
2 teaspoons sesame seeds

METHOD:

1. To make the sauce, whisk the soy sauce, honey, lemon juice and cornflour together in a small bowl.

2. Heat a wok over high heat until hot. Add half the oil and carefully swirl it around to coat the sides of the wok and heat until very hot.

3. Add half the prawns and stir-fry for 2–3 minutes until they change colour. Transfer to a plate and set aside. Repeat with the remaining prawns.

4. Heat the remaining oil in the wok over high heat. Add the broccoli, carrot and bok choy and stir-fry for 3–4 minutes until tender-crisp. Add the capsicum, garlic, ginger and chilli (if using), and stir-fry for a further 1–2 minutes.

5. Pour in the sauce and toss gently to coat the veggies. Add the prawns and stir-fry for 1–2 minutes or until the prawns are heated through. Meanwhile, pierce the noodle packet and microwave for 1 minute, to loosen and gently heat. Add the noodles and half the sesame seeds to the stir-fry and toss gently to combine.

6. To serve, place the stir-fry in a serving bowl and sprinkle over the remaining sesame seeds.

Tips

This dish is meal-prep friendly! Portion out leftovers and refrigerate them for a grab-and-go option that can be taken to school or work.

Use frozen veggies to save both money and prep time. Packed with as much nutrition as fresh, they're widely available and can help reduce food wastage too.

Greek Chicken Quinoa Salad

Prep time: 10 mins | **Cook time:** 12 mins | **Serves:** 1

Quinoa is a great option for a gluten-free grain and a source of important nutrients including fibre, zinc and antioxidants. The most time-consuming part of this dish is cooking the quinoa, but once you've done that it comes together super quickly with plenty of fresh, flavourful ingredients and leafy greens.

INGREDIENTS:

50 g quinoa
3 teaspoons olive oil
¼ teaspoon dried oregano
2 teaspoons lemon juice, to taste
sea salt and ground black pepper
100 g chicken breast fillet, sliced
4 cherry tomatoes, halved
¼ Lebanese cucumber, chopped
1 tablespoon diced red onion
4 kalamata olives, pitted and halved
1 small handful baby spinach leaves
20 g salt-reduced feta cheese, crumbled

METHOD:

1. To cook the quinoa, combine it with 1 cup (250 ml) water in a small saucepan and bring to the boil over high heat, stirring occasionally. Reduce the heat to low and simmer, covered, for 10–12 minutes, until the liquid is absorbed and the quinoa is tender. Transfer to a mixing bowl to cool.

2. Meanwhile, to make the dressing, combine 2 teaspoons of the olive oil, the oregano and the lemon juice in a small bowl and whisk to combine. Season with salt to taste.

3. In a separate bowl, toss the chicken with the remaining olive oil to evenly coat. Season with salt and pepper.

4. Heat a non-stick frying pan over medium-high heat and cook the chicken for 5–6 minutes (turning halfway), until browned and cooked through.

5. Add the cherry tomatoes, cucumber, onion, olives and spinach to the quinoa and toss gently to combine.

6. To serve, place the salad in a serving bowl and top with the chicken. Drizzle with the dressing and sprinkle over the feta.

Chicken and Vegetable Stir-fry

Prep time: 10 mins | **Cook time:** 25 mins | **Serves:** 4

Meal prepping is so helpful, but keeping it interesting and flavoursome is key to avoiding a recipe rut. Stir-fries make it easy – just switch up the vegetables, swap out your protein, and pack in flavour with plenty of garlic, ginger, soy sauce and sesame oil. Great for a fridge clean out too, just use up whatever you have on hand!

INGREDIENTS:

200 g brown rice
2 teaspoons sesame oil
500 g chicken breast
    fillet, sliced
1 zucchini, sliced
2 small red capsicum, sliced
2 small carrots, thinly sliced
1 small red onion,
    thinly sliced
3 garlic cloves, crushed
2 teaspoons finely grated
    fresh ginger
½ cup (125 ml) soy sauce
    or tamari
coriander leaves and sliced
    spring onion, to serve

METHOD:

1. Cook the rice according to packet instructions. Drain well.

2. Meanwhile, add 1 teaspoon of the sesame oil to a wok and heat over high heat. Stir-fry the chicken in 3 batches for 1–2 minutes or until browned and just cooked. Transfer to a plate and set aside.

3. Heat the remaining oil in the wok. Add the zucchini, capsicum, carrot and red onion, and stir-fry for 2 minutes. Add 1 tablespoon water and stir-fry for 1 minute more, until the vegetables are tender-crisp.

4. Add the garlic, ginger and soy sauce and stir continuously for 1–2 minutes, until fragrant. Return the cooked chicken to the wok, tossing to combine.

5. To serve, place the cooked rice into serving bowls and top with the chicken stir-fry. Garnish with the coriander leaves and sliced spring onion.

Tips

To save time, the rice can be cooked the night before and stored in an airtight container in the refrigerator. Reheat in the microwave.

Customise this recipe by swapping chicken for beef or tofu or adding different vegetables like broccoli or snow peas to suit your preferences. You can also swap the rice for your favourite noodles.

Tip
Burger patties can be frozen
for up to 2 months. Wrap
tightly in plastic film then
place into an airtight freezer
bag with the air expelled.

Easy Homemade Beef Burgers

Prep time: 25 mins | **Cook time:** 10 mins | **Serves:** 4

You know you've nailed a good homemade burger when it's better than takeaway, and this one is so good. For cheese lovers, my family tell me that melting the cheese is a must. If it's taking too long to melt, place a lid on the pan to speed things up. While the homemade burger sauce is optional, it's super easy and all you need is a few pantry staples.

INGREDIENTS:

500 g lean beef mince
1 small brown onion,
    finely chopped
2 garlic cloves, crushed
1 teaspoon Worcestershire
    sauce
½ teaspoon dried oregano
sea salt and ground
    black pepper
olive oil spray
80 g cheddar cheese, sliced
4 burger buns, halved
1 large handful iceberg
    or cos lettuce leaves
2 tomatoes, sliced

Burger sauce (optional):

100 g low-fat mayonnaise
1 tablespoon tomato sauce
    or ketchup
1 tablespoon Dijon mustard
1 teaspoon Worcestershire
    sauce
sea salt and ground
    black pepper

METHOD:

1. Combine the beef mince, onion, garlic, Worcestershire sauce and oregano in a mixing bowl and season with salt and pepper. Mix thoroughly to combine. Shape the mixture into 4 round patties, slightly larger in diameter than the burger buns (they will shrink during cooking).

2. Spray a large non-stick frying pan with oil and heat over medium-high heat. Cook the patties for 4–5 minutes each side or until cooked through. In the last minute of cooking, place cheese slices on each patty and allow them to melt.

3. Meanwhile, to make the optional burger sauce, combine the sauce ingredients in a small bowl and mix well. Season with salt and pepper to taste.

4. Toast the burger buns to your liking.

5. To serve, top each bun with the burger sauce (if using), a patty, lettuce leaves and tomatoes.

Homemade Pizza on Pita Bread

Prep time: 15 mins | **Cook time:** 10 mins | **Serves:** 2

Pita bread or wraps make the perfect instant base for pizzas, and they're such a good option if you're low on time or energy, or have kids in your house! These toppings are inspired by my love of salads with balsamic vinegar, but I know people are picky with pizza toppings, so get creative. Just don't forget the passata.

INGREDIENTS:

2 large pita breads or
  wholemeal wraps
100 g tomato passata
100 g mushrooms, stalks
  removed and sliced
1 tomato, diced
60 g mozzarella cheese,
  grated or sliced
1 tablespoon olive oil
2 teaspoons balsamic
  vinegar
pinch sea salt
1 small handful rocket leaves

METHOD:

1.   Preheat oven to 180°C (160°C fan-forced).
     Line a large baking tray with baking paper and
     place the pita breads on the prepared tray.

2.   Spread the pita breads with tomato passata.

3.   In a bowl, toss together the mushroom,
     tomato and cheese then distribute evenly
     over both pizzas.

4.   Bake for 8–10 minutes or until the toppings
     are hot, the cheese has melted and the edges
     are golden brown.

5.   Meanwhile, whisk the olive oil, balsamic vinegar
     and a pinch of sea salt in a small bowl.

6.   To serve, top the pizza with the rocket leaves
     and drizzle over the balsamic and olive oil dressing.

Chicken 'Yiros'

Prep time: 10 mins | **Cook time:** 12 mins | **Serves:** 2

Greek food is the best, and I love yiros nights with my family – even better when there's leftovers for the next day. This isn't a traditional yiros but it's so easy to whip together. It's tempting to cook the chicken at a super-high heat, but the key to keeping it juicy is to stick to a medium-high heat. I recommend taking the time to make homemade tzatziki, too!

INGREDIENTS:

150 g chicken breast fillet
2 teaspoons olive oil
½ teaspoon dried oregano
sea salt and ground
    black pepper
2 wholemeal wraps
Kayla's Tzatziki (see page 65)
4 lettuce leaves
1 tomato, diced
½ red onion, finely diced
½ Lebanese
    cucumber, diced
mint leaves, to serve
    (optional)

METHOD:

1. Cut the chicken breast into bite-sized portions and place in a small bowl. Add the olive oil and oregano and season with salt and pepper to taste.

2. Heat a non-stick frying pan over medium-high heat. Add the chicken and cook for 8–12 minutes or until the chicken is cooked through, stirring occasionally. Transfer to a bowl and set aside.

3. Heat the wraps in the microwave, or in a hot frying pan for 10–20 seconds on each side, if desired.

4. To serve, place the wraps on serving plates and spread with tzatziki. Place the lettuce, chicken, tomato, red onion and cucumber down the middle of each wrap and sprinkle with mint leaves (if using). Fold over the end of the wrap, then roll up to enclose the filling.

Vietnamese Noodle Bowl

Prep time: 15 mins | **Cook time:** 5 mins | **Serves:** 2

This Vietnamese-inspired dish is essentially a deconstructed rice paper roll, which I love because it's an easy throw-together meal with heaps of room for fresh and tasty ingredients (and it's very hard to get wrong). This version uses tofu, but if you prefer another protein, like beef mince, that will work well too.

INGREDIENTS:

100 g rice vermicelli noodles
olive oil spray
350 g firm tofu (or 130 g
    cubed chicken or pork)
2 carrots, peeled and grated
1 large Lebanese cucumber,
    finely sliced
1 small handful mint leaves
1 small handful coriander
    leaves
black or white sesame
    seeds, toasted, to serve
    (optional)

Dressing:

2 tablespoons fish sauce
2 tablespoons rice
    wine vinegar
2 teaspoons pure
    maple syrup
1 tablespoon lime juice,
    to taste
1 garlic clove, crushed
1 teaspoon finely chopped
    fresh red chilli

METHOD:

1. Place the noodles in a heatproof bowl and cover with boiling water. Leave for 10 minutes, then loosen the noodles with a fork. Drain and refresh under cool running water. Drain well and set aside to cool slightly.

2. Meanwhile, spray a non-stick frying pan with oil and heat over medium-high heat. Add the tofu (or protein of choice) and cook for 5 minutes or until golden brown, stirring occasionally.

3. To make the dressing, whisk the fish sauce, rice wine vinegar, maple syrup, lime juice, garlic, chilli and ⅓ cup (80 ml) water together in a small bowl.

4. Place the noodles, tofu, carrot, cucumber, mint and coriander in a mixing bowl. Drizzle over the dressing and toss gently to combine.

5. To serve, divide the salad between serving bowls and top with sesame seeds, if desired.

Baked Fish and Sweet Potato Fries

Prep time: 10 mins | **Cook time:** 30 mins | **Serves:** 2

Fish and chips are such a classic, especially if you've got young kids. If you have an air fryer, you can cook the sweet potato wedges in there (with a dash of smoked paprika for extra flavour) to save time while you cook the rest. I'm not a fan of complicated cooking, and this all comes together quickly in the oven without needing to keep an eye on multiple pans.

INGREDIENTS:

1 sweet potato, cut into
   1 cm thick wedges
1 tablespoon olive oil
1 teaspoon smoked paprika
sea salt and ground
   black pepper
1 lemon, half juiced and
   half sliced
1 teaspoon chopped parsley
1 teaspoon chopped
   oregano
250 g white fish fillets

METHOD:

1. Preheat oven to 200°C (180°C fan-forced) and line 2 baking trays with baking paper.

2. Combine the sweet potato, 2 teaspoons of the olive oil and the smoked paprika in a mixing bowl. Season with salt and mix with your hands to coat the sweet potato evenly with seasoning. Spread the sweet potato fries in a single layer on one of the baking trays.

3. Bake for 15 minutes then remove and turn the pieces over with tongs. Return to the oven to cook for another 15 minutes or until golden brown.

4. Meanwhile, whisk the lemon juice, remaining olive oil and herbs together in a small bowl.

5. Place the fish fillets onto the other baking tray. Drizzle over the lemon and herb mixture and season with salt and pepper.

6. Bake the fish for 10–15 minutes or until it is opaque and flakes easily with a fork.

7. To serve, place the baked fish on serving plates with a side of sweet potato fries and sliced lemon.

Sticky Beef and Rice Bowl

Prep time: 15 mins | **Cook time:** 25 mins | **Serves:** 2

Every bite of this bowl is the perfect blend of spicy and sweet thanks to its mix of honey and chilli flakes, and being so colourful and fresh, it's easy to make look impressive. For extra protein and to really bring it together, I love adding an egg on top too.

INGREDIENTS:

60 g brown rice
2 teaspoons sesame oil
1 red capsicum, julienned
1 carrot, julienned
160 g snow peas, trimmed
170 g lean beef, sliced
    into strips
2 teaspoons sesame seeds
2 large eggs
½ avocado, sliced
1 spring onion, sliced
1 long red chilli, sliced
    diagonally

Sticky sweet chilli sauce:

2 tablespoons honey
2 tablespoons soy sauce
1 tablespoon rice
    wine vinegar
2 teaspoons sesame oil
1 tablespoon cornflour
½ teaspoon chilli flakes

METHOD:

1. Place the rice and ½ cup (125 ml) water in a small saucepan over high heat and bring to the boil, stirring occasionally. Reduce the heat to low and simmer, covered, for 25 minutes or until the liquid has been absorbed and the rice is tender. Remove from the heat and leave to stand, covered, for 5 minutes.

2. Meanwhile, to make the sticky sweet chilli sauce, whisk all the ingredients together in a small bowl.

3. Heat the sesame oil in a medium non-stick frying pan over high heat. Add the capsicum, carrot and snow peas and stir-fry for 3–4 minutes or until tender-crisp. Transfer to a bowl and set aside.

4. Reheat the pan over high heat. Add the beef strips and stir-fry for 2–3 minutes or until browned and cooked to your liking. Pour over the sauce, allowing it to coat the beef. For extra saucy beef, add ¼ cup water to the pan. Cook for a further 2–3 minutes or until the sauce has thickened, stirring frequently, then sprinkle over the sesame seeds. Transfer to a bowl and set aside to rest.

5. Wipe the pan clean and reheat over medium heat. Crack the eggs into the pan and cook them for 1–2 minutes or until the whites are opaque and the yolk is set to your liking.

6. To serve, place the rice into a serving bowl and top with the sticky beef, capsicum, carrot, snow peas, avocado and egg. Garnish with spring onion and fresh chilli.

Lemon Garlic and Roasted Tomato Pasta

Prep time: 10 mins | **Cook time:** 20 mins | **Serves:** 2

Roasted tomatoes are one of my favourite ways to add flavour to pasta dishes in a way no jar of sauce can! It takes almost as long to cook the pasta as roast the veggies, so you may as well – the extra flavour is so worth it! I use plenty of garlic here, so if you can, always go for fresh cloves, and don't forget the lemon – it's not the same without it.

INGREDIENTS:

1 large red capsicum, chopped
250 g cherry tomatoes
¼ cup (60 ml) olive oil
sea salt and ground black pepper
200 g dried pasta (gluten-free if desired)
4 garlic cloves
1 lemon, zest finely grated, juiced
chilli flakes, to taste
chopped basil or parsley, to serve

METHOD:

1. Preheat oven to 200°C (180°C fan-forced) and line a baking tray with baking paper.

2. Combine the vegetables and 1 tablespoon of oil in a medium bowl and toss gently to coat. Season with salt and pepper to taste. Transfer the vegetables to the baking tray in a single layer and bake for 15–20 minutes, until lightly roasted. Remove from the oven and set aside.

3. Meanwhile, cook the pasta according to packet instructions or until al dente (the pasta will continue cooking slightly in later steps so do not overcook). Drain and set aside.

4. Heat a large non-stick frying pan over medium heat and add remaining oil. Add the garlic and cook for 1 minute or until fragrant, stirring constantly.

5. Add the cooked pasta, lemon zest, juice and chilli flakes. Season with salt and pepper. Mix gently to combine and heat through for 2–3 minutes. Fold the roasted vegetables through.

6. To serve, divide between bowls and sprinkle with basil or parsley.

Pita Triangles with Hummus

Prep time: 10 mins | **Cook time:** 10 mins | **Serves:** 2

RECIPES

This is my favourite way to use up any leftover pita breads or wraps, and with the hummus it's such a delicious snack that you can keep in your fridge and pantry for a few days, or easily take with you on the go.

INGREDIENTS:

2 wholemeal pita bread
    or gluten-free wraps,
    cut into wedges
olive oil spray
160 g tinned chickpeas,
    rinsed and drained
1 tablespoon tahini
1 tablespoon olive oil
1 garlic clove
½ teaspoon ground cumin
sea salt and ground
    black pepper

METHOD:

1. Preheat oven to 200°C (180°C fan-forced) and line 2 baking trays with baking paper.

2. Lay the pita wedges in a single layer on the lined baking trays and spray lightly with oil. Bake for 5 minutes or until they begin to colour. Turn the wedges over and bake for a further 5 minutes or until both sides are lightly coloured and set aside to cool.

3. To make the hummus, place the chickpeas, tahini, olive oil, garlic and cumin in a food processor or small blender and pulse until smooth. Season with salt and pepper to taste.

4. Serve the pita triangles with the hummus.

Tip

To save time, the dip can be made the night before and stored in an airtight container in the refrigerator.

Kayla's Tzatziki

Prep time: 10 mins + overnight draining (optional)

Tzatziki is a key ingredient in many of my favourite Greek dishes, and trust me, no store-bought version is as good as making your own. It may seem like a lot of steps with the straining and refrigeration, but it's actually super simple and makes all the difference to getting it really thick and creamy.

INGREDIENTS:

300 g Greek-style yoghurt
¼ teaspoon sea salt
1 Lebanese cucumber, grated
2–3 garlic cloves, crushed
lemon juice, to taste
1 tablespoon olive oil
chopped herbs such as mint or dill (optional)
sea salt and ground black pepper

METHOD:

1. Place the yoghurt into a medium bowl and stir in the salt.

2. Line a colander with 3–4 layers of cheesecloth (or similar) and place the colander over a deep medium bowl. Pour the yoghurt into the cheesecloth. Gather all sides of the cheesecloth together and secure it with a rubber band.

3. Place the bowl in the refrigerator for 12–24 hours. This process will allow the liquid (whey) to drain from the yoghurt. The longer it drains, the thicker the tzatziki will be.

4. Open the cheesecloth and scoop the yoghurt into a medium bowl.

5. Once the drained yoghurt is ready, prepare the cucumber. Using your hands or a strainer, squeeze out the excess liquid from the cucumber.

6. Add the cucumber, garlic, lemon juice and olive oil to the drained yoghurt. Add the herbs, if using, and season with salt and pepper. Mix well to combine.

7. Use immediately or store in an airtight container in the fridge for up to 1 week.

Tip
Straining the yoghurt overnight is an optional step, but it makes the dip thicker and allows it to develop a tangier flavour. Skip this step if you are running short on time! Serve this dip with anything from cut veggies to crackers or falafel for an easy snack.

Chilli and Lime Baked Chickpeas

Prep time: 10 mins | **Cook time:** 40 mins | **Serves:** 4

Chickpeas are versatile, cheap, nutritious and make such a great snack. The seasoning here is what makes them so good, and you can easily use them as a topping on main meals or as a side dish. Simply drain, toss in the seasoning and roast – that's it!

INGREDIENTS:

1 tablespoon olive oil
½ tablespoon smoked paprika
1 teaspoon ground cumin
¼ teaspoon chilli powder
¼ teaspoon ground turmeric
¼ teaspoon sea salt
½ lime, juiced
400 g tin chickpeas, rinsed and drained

METHOD:

1. Preheat oven to 200°C (180°C fan-forced) and line a rimmed baking tray with baking paper.

2. Combine the olive oil, paprika, cumin, chilli powder, turmeric, salt and lime juice in a bowl.

3. Add the chickpeas and stir well to coat them evenly in the spice mixture, then spread in an even layer on the lined baking tray.

4. Bake chickpeas for 30–40 minutes or until golden and crispy. Check them halfway and give them a stir to make sure they roast evenly.

5. Allow the chickpeas to cool and crisp up before eating. These chickpeas will store in an airtight container for up to 2 days.

Tip
Eat these alone as a delicious snack or add them to salads for extra crunch and texture.

Sweet Toast Toppers

Prep time: 5 mins | **Cook time:** 5 mins | **Serves:** 1

Toast is such an underrated snack. If you go for a wholegrain variety, it's high in fibre and vitamins, plus all the nutrients and flavour in your toppings. These topping ideas are a quick way to get some extra fruit into your day and give you plenty of options whenever you're stuck for snack ideas.

INGREDIENTS:

1 slice wholemeal or gluten-free bread

Topping ideas:

½ banana, sliced + 1 tablespoon ricotta cheese + ground cinnamon

10 blueberries + 1 tablespoon cream cheese + drizzle of honey

2 strawberries, sliced + 1 tablespoon almond or cashew butter + shredded coconut

METHOD:

1. Toast the bread to your liking.

2. Top the toast with your desired toppings and serve.

Double Choc Bliss Balls

Prep time: 20 mins + 50 mins chilling | **Serves:** 16

For those mid-afternoon sweet cravings, bliss balls are a staple. They're so quick to make, taste amazing, cater to lots of dietary requirements and will give you an energy boost. To prep for the week, mix these together on a Sunday so you've got a supply of snacks whenever you need.

INGREDIENTS:

For the base:

100 g unsalted cashews
10 medjool dates, pitted, chopped
¼ cup cacao powder
2 tablespoons almond butter
¼ teaspoon sea salt

For the raw chocolate coating:

50 g coconut oil, melted
1 tablespoon pure maple syrup
1 ½ tablespoons cacao powder

METHOD:

1. Line a baking tray with baking paper.

2. Place all of the base ingredients into a food processor and process for 5–7 minutes, until the mixture thickens and sticks to the sides of the bowl, scraping down the sides occasionally. It should become smooth and shiny as the natural oils of the nuts are released.

3. Use wet hands to roll heaped tablespoons of the mixture into balls. Place onto the lined tray and refrigerate for 30 minutes.

4. To make the raw chocolate coating, whisk the melted coconut oil, maple syrup and cacao powder in a small mixing bowl. Ensure that the cacao powder has dissolved completely.

5. Roll the bliss balls in the coating and return to the baking tray. Refrigerate for 20 minutes until the chocolate shell is firm. Store in an airtight container in the refrigerator for up to 1 week.

Banana Peanut Butter Chia Pudding

Prep time: 10 mins + overnight chilling | **Serves:** 2

If you love banana and peanut butter, I bet this will quickly become part of your snack or breakfast rotation! It's an easy prep-ahead meal – all you need to do is mix the ingredients together and chill it overnight before topping with peanut butter and banana.

INGREDIENTS:

4 tablespoons chia seeds
1 cup (250 ml) unsweetened
    coconut milk
30 g low-fat plain yoghurt
    (or coconut yoghurt)
1 tablespoon pure
    maple syrup
¼ teaspoon ground
    cinnamon
pinch salt
2 tablespoons peanut butter
1 banana, sliced

METHOD:

1. Place the chia seeds, milk, yoghurt, maple syrup, cinnamon and salt in a bowl and mix until well combined. Pour the mixture into 2 glass jars or containers of your choice.

2. Cover with plastic film or lids and place in the refrigerator to chill overnight.

3. To serve, top the chia pudding with peanut butter and sliced banana.

EXERCISES

GETTING STARTED

It doesn't matter whether you're at the start of your fitness journey, you've been training for years or you're coming back from a break, the Sweat team and I are huge believers that there is so much confidence to be found in movement – for *everyone*.

Alongside how empowering it can be to put your wellbeing first and feel your fitness and strength build, there are so many amazing reasons to fall in love with movement. At Sweat, we want to make it as easy as possible for you to invest in yourself and your health.

When I'm moving my body regularly, I find the quality of my sleep is better, my energy and focus is sharper, my skin looks healthier, my confidence is higher, my ability to deal with stress improves and I feel a whole lot happier. As clichéd as it sounds, training helps me be a better friend, sister, daughter, mother, partner and businesswoman.

I'm all for setting goals, and they can be an amazing way to get started, keep yourself going and have moments to celebrate. But as your trainer, what makes me even more excited is that moment when you get a sense of just how good fitness can make you *feel*.

If you're at the start of your fitness journey (or are hitting reboot after some time off), it's okay if feeling good about exercise isn't your main source of motivation right now. It doesn't matter whether we're talking about fitness or life in general – big, positive changes can often begin with feeling unhappy about something in your life and the sense that a shift is needed.

You might be motivated to work out in Week 1 because you're sick of not feeling confident in your body or because something in your life isn't going right. But by Week 4, I hope you'll be working out because of how good it makes you feel. That's just how Sweat works.

Aside from your workouts, I want to take you through a few of my fitness fundamentals to set you up for success, and create the kind of relationship with fitness where you genuinely look forward to moving your body – where Sweat is what makes you feel like the best version of you.

EXERCISE TIPS

THE ESSENTIAL TEN

01. FORM COMES FIRST

You can be an absolute beginner or an elite athlete, but lifting heavy, speeding through your workouts or trying advanced exercises is a waste of time (and a recipe for injury) if your form isn't correct. That's why we've included instructions alongside each exercise in your movement plan. Focusing on getting your form right should be your priority, so go at whatever pace, difficulty level or weight will ensure you feel challenged while still getting the most out of every rep.

02. DON'T BE AFRAID TO USE SUBSTITUTE EXERCISES

A common fitness myth I want to bust is that substituting an exercise or changing part of your workout means you're not fit or strong enough. Exercise should feel good, and that's the whole point of substitutions. You might swap out jumping exercises if you have bad knees, your best friend might not enjoy burpees if she has a big bust, or your sister might change an exercise simply because she'd rather do something else. I want you to feel empowered to make your workouts work for you!

03. DRINK UP AND FUEL UP!

As much as exercising can *give* you energy, it also *needs* energy, and getting into a good fitness routine goes hand-in-hand with eating nourishing foods. The timing and size of your meals and snacks in relation to your workouts is different for everyone and it might take some experimentation to find your sweet spot, but aim to eat enough and drink plenty of water to perform at your best.

04. LOVE HOW YOU CHOOSE TO MOVE

I've always loved HIIT (high-intensity interval training) workouts for how they make me feel and I know so many women in the Sweat Community love this training style too. Find the style of movement that makes *you* feel your best. It might be yoga, boxing, team sports, Pilates, heavy lifting or a combination of styles. Or it may change over time! Any time I hear someone say they don't enjoy exercise, I genuinely believe they just haven't found something they enjoy yet.

05. PREPARATION IS KEY

Although you can't talk or think yourself fit, there's definitely something to be said for the power of preparation. Workout prep can range from choosing your activewear, packing your gym bag or previewing your Sweat session in advance, to planning your entire week of workouts, creating a playlist or having a pre-workout snack in your bag.

06. FIND THE BEST TIME FOR *YOU*

I'm often asked, *when is the best time to work out?* The short answer is: whenever it works for your body, energy levels and schedule. My guess is that you've already got more than enough to juggle in your life, so do yourself a huge favour and move when it suits you. Getting it done matters far more than *when* you get it done.

07. DON'T COMPARE YOURSELF

Despite all the inspiring women around the world who are on their own health and fitness journeys alongside you, your path is yours and yours alone. No one else lives the life you live or has the goals you have, and that is your power! Forget about wasting energy on comparison and run your own race. You'll feel so much better for it.

08. KNOW WHICH INNER VOICE YOU'RE LISTENING TO

Listening to your body can help you to avoid burnout and injury, train with your menstrual cycle, or know when to step up your training, but be wary of it becoming an excuse for the times you don't feel like working out or putting in effort. Listening to your body is great advice, but make sure you're being honest and challenging yourself too.

09. CELEBRATE EVERY SMALL WIN

The one thing I regret in my fitness journey is not celebrating more often. As rewarding as your fitness journey will be, that doesn't mean it's going to feel easy every day. Some days a five-minute workout will feel like a massive achievement, but other days you might find yourself smashing a goal in the gym with ease. It's *all* worth celebrating, so look for every win you can get excited about.

10. HAVE YOUR NEXT GOAL READY

One of the easiest ways to lose momentum is to only have one goal in mind. Once you achieve it, you stop because you didn't make a plan for what's next. As you set each goal or get close to achieving it, start to plan your next one to keep yourself going!

FITNESS FUNDAMENTALS

While you might have short-term goals to keep you motivated, the best approach is to think about fitness as a lifelong pursuit. When your focus is only on a single goal or the next few weeks ahead, it's easy to smash out your workouts and neglect the essentials that keep your body strong, mobile and injury-free.

If these fundamentals feel less exciting to you, think of them as ways to give some love back to your body every day when you're asking so much of it with each workout. Throughout your four-week reboot, making these elements a priority will set you up to be fit for *life*.

WARM UP

If you want to feel your best during your workout and get the most out of it, never skip your warm-up. Especially before high-intensity exercise, warming up is so important to gradually increase your blood flow, heart rate and body temperature, preparing your muscles for the movement to come and reducing your risk of injury. A few minutes of cardio makes a great warm-up, along with some dynamic stretching to get your muscles and joints moving. Prioritising your warm-up can boost your performance and overall fitness results!

COOL DOWN

We get it – at the end of your workout, you want to wrap it up and get out of there ASAP. So, when it comes to cooling down, we're not asking you to do a 15-minute stretching session, but to gradually bring your breathing and heart rate back to normal with a few minutes of light cardio or gentle stretching (or both!). A short cool-down can help you to avoid any post-workout light-headedness, as well as promote faster recovery for your next session.

MOBILITY AND RECOVERY

In five, 10 or 50 years' time, you don't want to feel stiff and held back by injuries – you want to be active, strong and moving with confidence. That means making recovery and mobility exercises a focus in your routine now. Mobility focuses on improving joint flexibility, stability and muscular control for optimal movement.

Including mobility exercises in your warm-up or cool-down is a great idea, or these can be performed as a standalone session on your rest days. We've included a range of mobility exercises in the book to get you started. Stretching, foam rolling and getting enough rest every week are also simple habits you can start today that will pay you back tenfold in years to come.

LISS

Low-intensity steady state (LISS) cardio can help improve endurance, cardiovascular health and energy burn while being gentle on the body, making it a sustainable way to move your body throughout every stage of life, and a great way to stay active on days when you don't have a workout. Walking is one of the most popular and accessible forms of LISS (check out more on getting your steps up in Week 2), but do whatever you enjoy most! Hop on a bike or a rowing or elliptical machine, or go for a swim.

BUTTERFLY STRETCH
BODY AREA: LOWER BODY

The butterfly stretch helps to open up the hips, stretch the inner thighs, and improve flexibility in the groin area. It is beneficial for increasing mobility in the hip joints and can help relieve tension and tightness in the hips and lower back.

1. Start by sitting on a yoga mat with your legs extended in front of you.

2. Release and turn out both legs, bringing the soles of your feet together directly in front of you. Your knees should be bent and pointing outwards, forming a diamond shape with your legs. ❶

3. Place your hands on your feet, resting your forearms on your thighs. Keep your spine straight and your shoulders relaxed.

4. Inhale to prepare. Exhale as you gently bend forward from the hips, lowering your torso towards the mat. Use your forearms to press your thighs down towards the mat, feeling a stretch in your inner thighs and groin area. ❷

5. Hold this position for the specified amount of time, breathing deeply throughout.

6. With each exhale, you can gradually lower your torso further towards the floor and use your forearms to press your thighs down, deepening the stretch.

Kayla's Tip
Take a deep breath in and then, as you breathe out, push your elbows further into your knees.

GLUTE STRETCH
BODY AREA: LOWER BODY

The glute stretch is beneficial for increasing flexibility in the gluteal muscles, increasing mobility in the hips, and relieving tightness and tension in the hips, buttocks and lower back.

1. Start by lying flat on your back on a yoga mat. Bend your knees and position your feet firmly on the mat, hip-width apart with your spine in a neutral position.

2. Release and turn out your left leg so that your left ankle is resting on your right leg just above your knee. ❶

3. Draw your right knee in towards your torso, resting both hands on the back of your right thigh. ❷

4. Hold this position for the specified amount of time, breathing deeply throughout.

5. Each time that you exhale, try to draw your knee further into your chest and press your left elbow into your left knee to increase the stretch, ensuring that your spine remains in a neutral position and your tailbone on the floor.

6. Repeat this stretch on the other side.

Kayla's Tip
If you can't feel much of a stretch, use one of your hands to apply outward pressure to the top leg being stretched.

HAMSTRING STRETCH
BODY AREA: LOWER BODY

The hamstring stretch helps to improve flexibility in the hamstrings, and increase mobility and relieve tightness in the hips and lower back.

1. While seated on a yoga mat, extend both legs out in front of you.

2. Release and turn out your left leg and place your foot on the inside of your right thigh. **1**

3. Bending from the hips, reach for your right foot (or as far as you can). If you can reach your toes, gently pull them back towards you, or rest your hands on your ankle or shin – whichever is most comfortable. **2**

4. Hold this position for the specified amount of time, breathing deeply throughout.

5. Each time that you exhale, try to lower your torso further towards your legs, ensuring that you are bending from the hips and not rounding through your spine.

6. Repeat this stretch on the other side.

Kayla's Tip
Hinging forward at the hips rather than rounding your back can help enhance the stretch on your hamstrings.

HIP FLEXOR STRETCH
BODY AREA: LOWER BODY

The hip flexor stretch helps to improve flexibility and mobility in the hips and thighs. It can also help alleviate tension and discomfort in these areas.

1. Begin in a kneeling position on a yoga mat.

2. Release your right leg and take a large step forward, bringing your right foot in front of you in a lunge position. Ensure that your right knee is not further forward than your toes.

3. Keep your torso upright and aligned with your hips.

4. Push your hips forward gently, feeling a stretch along the front of your left leg.

5. Hold this position for the specified amount of time, focusing on deep breathing.

6. As you exhale, engage your abdominal muscles and gently tuck your pubic bone towards your belly button to increase the stretch in the hip flexors.

7. Repeat this stretch on the other side.

Kayla's Tip
Tuck your hips under and push forward into the front knee, keeping your torso tall to enhance the stretch.

PIRIFORMIS STRETCH (CHAIR)
BODY AREA: LOWER BODY

The piriformis stretch helps to target the piriformis muscle, which is located deep in the glutes. Stretching this muscle can be beneficial for relieving tightness and tension in the hips and buttocks, particularly for individuals who experience piriformis syndrome or general hip tightness.

1. Begin by sitting on a chair or bench with your feet flat on the floor, hip-width apart, and your spine in a neutral position.

2. Place your left ankle on top of your right knee, allowing your left knee to drop out to the side. Your left foot should be flexed to protect your ankle.

3. This is your starting position for the piriformis stretch on the left side.

4. As you exhale, gently add pressure to your left thigh, pushing it downward. You should feel a deep stretch in your left glute and outer hip. Be mindful not to push to the point of pain; the stretch should be comfortable and manageable. ①

5. Hold this position for the specified amount of time, continuing to breathe deeply throughout the stretch.

6. To release the stretch, slowly remove the pressure from your thigh and bring your left foot back to the floor.

7. Repeat the same sequence on the opposite side by placing your right ankle on top of your left knee and adding gentle pressure to your right thigh.

Kayla's Tip

Apply pressure gently, taking deep breaths to relax prior to stretching further.

QUAD STRETCH
BODY AREA: LOWER BODY

The quad stretch is used to improve flexibility in your quadricep muscles, which are the muscles located on the front of your thighs. It can also help to alleviate tightness and discomfort in this area.

1. Begin standing with your feet slightly further than shoulder-width apart.

2. Bend your left knee and bring your foot back directly behind you towards your glute so that you can hold it with your hand. You should feel a stretch in the front of your left leg. ①

3. Hold this position for the specified amount of time. If you're struggling to balance, focus on a spot directly ahead of you or extend your right arm for support.

4. Repeat this stretch with your right leg.

Kayla's Tip
Use a wall or a chair for support if balancing is too difficult.

90/90 WIPERS
BODY AREA: LOWER BODY

The 90/90 wipers exercise helps to improve hip mobility, strengthen the core, and increase flexibility in the lower body.

1. Start by sitting on the floor with one leg bent in front of your body and the other leg bent to the side. Both hips and knees should be at a 90-degree angle.

2. Ensure that your torso is upright and your hands are resting behind you for support. This is your starting position. ①

3. Keep your feet on the floor and maintain a neutral spine and engaged core.

4. Lift both knees off the ground simultaneously and swivel your hips, allowing your knees to move to the opposite side of your body. ② ③ ④

5. Aim to keep your glutes in contact with the ground throughout the movement.

6. Stay in control, moving through your full range of motion, feeling a stretch in your hips and lower body.

7. Alternate between sides, bringing your knees from one side to the other, for the specified amount of time or number of repetitions.

8. Focus on maintaining stability and control throughout the exercise, engaging your core and keeping your movements smooth and controlled.

Kayla's Tip
This one's great for anyone who has sore or tight hips.

DEEP SQUAT AND ROTATION
BODY AREA: LOWER BODY

The deep squat and rotation exercise helps to improve mobility in the hips and spine, strengthen the core, and increase flexibility in the lower body.

1. Start by standing with your feet slightly wider than shoulder-width apart. This is your starting position.

2. Inhale, then, as you exhale, bend at both the hips and knees to lower into a squat, ensuring that your knees remain in line with your toes. Continue bending your knees, aiming to have your upper legs slightly below parallel to the floor. Maintain a straight back and engage your core. ①

3. While maintaining this deep squat position, reach your right arm upwards, lengthening your spine and rotating your torso towards your right knee. Turn your eyes towards your right hand. Press your left elbow gently into the inner left thigh to feel a stretch in the inner thigh and hip. ②

4. Inhale as you untwist your torso and return to the centre.

5. Exhale as you repeat the rotation on the other side. Reach your left arm upwards, lengthen your spine, and rotate your torso towards your left knee. Turn your eyes towards your left hand. Press your right elbow gently into the inner right thigh to feel a stretch in the inner thigh and hip. ③

6. Inhale as you untwist your torso and return both arms to a neutral position.

7. Exhale and return to standing in the starting position.

8. Repeat the deep squat and rotation for the specified amount of time or number of repetitions.

Kayla's Tip
Keep your knees out and rotate at your torso.

HIP FLEXOR TO HAMSTRING
BODY AREA: LOWER BODY

The hip flexor to hamstring stretch helps to improve flexibility and mobility in the hips, thighs and hamstrings. It can also help alleviate tightness and discomfort in these areas.

1. Start in a kneeling position on a yoga mat.

2. Release your right leg and take a large step forward, ensuring that your right knee is not further forward than your toes. Keep your torso upright and engage your core. This is your starting position.

3. Inhale to prepare. Exhale as you shift your weight forward, pushing your hips forward and feeling a stretch in the front of your left hip and thigh. Keep your torso upright and maintain proper alignment of your knee and ankle. 1

4. Hold this hip flexor stretch for three to five seconds, breathing deeply throughout.

5. Inhale to prepare. Exhale as you shift your weight back, straightening your right leg and flexing your toes towards your body. Keep your shoulders and hips level and avoid rounding your back. 2

6. Hold this hamstring stretch for three to five seconds, feeling the stretch in the back of your right leg, and continue breathing deeply.

7. Inhale to prepare. Exhale as you bend your right knee, pressing your toes into the mat and lifting your torso away from your right thigh. Maintain an upright posture and engage your core.

8. Hold this position for three to five seconds, continuing to breathe deeply.

9. Continue alternating between the hip flexor stretch and hamstring stretch positions for the specified amount of time.

10. Repeat the entire sequence on the other side, starting with the left leg forward.

Kayla's Tip
Make sure to do this before your workout.

CHILD'S POSE
BODY AREA: UPPER BODY

Child's pose is a restorative posture that helps to calm the mind, relieve stress, and gently stretch the muscles of the back, hips and shoulders. It is often used as a resting position during yoga practice or as a gentle stretch to release tension in the body.

1. Start on all fours, with your hands shoulder-width apart and your knees hip-width apart. Your toes can be untucked.

2. Slowly shift your weight back towards your heels, drawing your glutes towards your heels.

3. Lower your torso down towards your thighs, allowing your forehead to rest on the mat. Your arms should be extended forward, resting on the mat in front of you. ①

4. Keep your arms active by pressing your palms into the mat and extending your fingertips forward.

5. Relax your shoulders and let them gently sink towards the mat, creating space between your shoulders and ears.

6. Breathe deeply and fully, allowing your breath to flow into your back body and ribcage.

7. Hold this position for the specified amount of time, focusing on deepening your breath and allowing your body to relax and release tension.

Kayla's Tip
No tip — this is just one of my favourite stretches.

NECK STRETCH (CHAIR)
BODY AREA: UPPER BODY

The neck stretch can help relieve tension and stiffness in the neck and upper trapezius muscles, which can be caused by prolonged sitting, poor posture or stress. It is important to perform the stretch gently and avoid any movements that cause discomfort. If you have any existing neck conditions or injuries, consult with a healthcare professional before attempting this stretch.

1. Start by sitting on a chair or bench with your feet planted firmly on the floor slightly wider than shoulder-width apart. Place your left hand under your backside, creating a stable base.

2. Relax your shoulders and keep your spine upright in a neutral position. This is your starting position.

3. Place your right hand on the side of your head, gently applying pressure to bring your right ear toward your right shoulder. Be sure to avoid pulling or jerking motions; the stretch should be gentle and controlled. ①

4. You should feel a gentle stretch along the left side of your neck and the upper trapezius muscle. It's important to listen to your body and avoid any pain or discomfort during the stretch.

5. Hold the stretch for the specified amount of time, breathing deeply and maintaining a relaxed posture.

6. To release the stretch, slowly bring your head back to an upright position and lower your right hand.

7. Repeat the same sequence on the opposite side by placing your right hand under your backside and using your left hand to bring your left ear toward your left shoulder.

Kayla's Tip
Be cautious and careful; slow is best.

TRICEP STRETCH
BODY AREA: UPPER BODY

The tricep stretch is used to improve flexibility in your tricep muscles, which are the muscles located on the back of your upper arms. It can also help to alleviate tightness and discomfort in this area.

1. Stand with your feet hip-width apart and arms by your sides.

2. Inhale, and as you exhale, raise your left arm overhead and bend it so that your hand reaches down between your shoulder blades.

3. With your right hand, gently push down on your left elbow. ①

4. Hold this position for the specified amount of time, breathing deeply.

5. Repeat the stretch on the other side.

Kayla's Tip
Make sure to stand nice and tall.

CAT-COW
BODY AREA: UPPER BODY

The cat-cow exercise helps to increase flexibility and mobility in the spine, as well as releasing tension in the neck and shoulders.

1. Start on all fours on a yoga mat, with your knees below your hips and your hands below your shoulders.

2. Set your spine in a neutral position, aligning your head, neck and back.

3. Inhale, then draw your shoulder blades down and back, engaging your core by gently drawing your belly button towards your spine.

4. Exhale slowly and press your hands and knees into the mat. Draw your chin towards your chest and round your spine, pulling your stomach in. This is the cat pose. ❶

5. Inhale deeply and slowly lift your chin, allowing your stomach to sink towards the floor. Arch your back and create space between your shoulders and ears. This is the cow pose. ❷

6. Flow between the cat and cow poses, moving with your breath. Exhale as you transition into cat, and inhale as you transition into cow.

7. Repeat this fluid movement for the specified amount of time, focusing on maintaining proper alignment and deepening the stretch with each repetition.

Kayla's Tip
Breathe in as you arch your back, breathe out as you round your back.

FLOOR SLIDES
BODY AREA: UPPER BODY

The floor slides exercise helps to improve shoulder mobility, strengthen the muscles around the shoulder blades, and promote proper shoulder mechanics.

1. Start by lying flat on your back, ensuring your spine is in a neutral position.

2. Place your hands next to your head, close to or touching the floor, with your palms facing up and your elbows bent at approximately 90 degrees. Draw your shoulder blades down and back. This is your starting position. 1

3. Inhale, then as you exhale, slowly slide your forearms along the floor, extending your arms straight overhead. Keep your hands and wrists close to or touching the floor throughout the movement. 2

4. Focus on maintaining control and feeling your shoulder blades squeezing together and down throughout the entire motion.

5. Inhale as you reverse the movement and slide your forearms back to the starting position. 3

6. Repeat for the specified number of repetitions.

EXERCISES

Kayla's Tip
Make sure to keep your fingertips close to or on the ground.

FOUR-POINT THORACIC ROTATION
BODY AREA: UPPER BODY

The four-point thoracic rotation exercise helps to improve mobility and flexibility in the thoracic spine, promoting better posture and reducing the risk of upper back and neck pain.

1. Begin on all fours with your knees below your hips and your hands below your shoulders. Maintain a neutral spine and engage your core muscles.

2. Inhale, then as you exhale, slowly rotate your torso, bringing your left elbow towards your right elbow. Keep your lower body stable.

3. Hold this rotated position for approximately three to five seconds, feeling a gentle stretch in your upper back and thoracic spine. Breathe deeply throughout the hold.

4. Inhale as you slowly rotate your torso to open your chest and point your hand towards the ceiling, or as far as you can while maintaining a neutral spine and keeping your lower body as still as possible.

5. After holding this position for approximately three to five seconds, repeat the rotation.

6. Complete half of the specified number of repetitions or time on the same side, then switch to the other side to complete the remaining repetitions or time.

Kayla's Tip
Perform these slowly and with control – don't swing through using momentum.

LYING THORACIC ROTATION
BODY AREA: UPPER BODY

The lying thoracic rotation exercise helps to improve mobility and flexibility in the thoracic spine, promoting better posture and reducing the risk of upper back and neck pain.

1. Start by lying on your side with your hands together and extended directly in front of your chest. Keep your head in line with your spine.

2. Bend your legs so that your hips and knees are at a 90-degree angle in front of you. Ensure that your hips are stacked and maintain a small gap between your waist and the floor. This is your starting position. ①

3. Inhale, and as you exhale, keeping your lower body as still as possible, release your top hand and rotate your torso away from your lower arm. Draw your lower shoulder towards the floor and allow your top arm to rotate with your torso until the top of your hand is resting on the floor or as close as is comfortable. ② ③

4. Inhale and rotate your arm and torso back towards your resting arm to return to the starting position.

5. Complete for the specified number of repetitions or time on each side.

Kayla's Tip
Good for anyone with a stiff back. Make sure to do this stretch before and after your workout.

SIT SQUAT (CHAIR)
BODY AREA: LOWER BODY

1. Place a chair or bench behind you and stand with your feet hip-width apart. This is your starting position.

2. Inhale, and looking straight ahead, bend at both the hips and knees to lower into a squat, ensuring that your knees remain in line with your toes.

3. Continue bending your knees and pushing your hips back until you sit on the chair behind you. **2**

4. Maintain a neutral spine and allow your torso to dip forward slightly. Lean back slightly to sit up tall once you have made contact with the chair.

5. Exhale, and while maintaining a neutral spine, lean forward slightly and push through your heels to extend your legs, stand tall and return to the starting position. **3**

6. Repeat for the specified number of repetitions.

Kayla's Tip
Keep your knees out and in line with your toes. Move with control rather than falling onto the chair or using momentum to stand up.

SQUAT
BODY AREA: LOWER BODY

1. Stand with your feet shoulder-width apart. This is your starting position.

2. Inhale and look straight ahead.

3. Bend at both the hips and knees to lower into a squat, ensuring that your knees remain in line with your toes.

4. Continue bending your knees, aiming to have your upper legs parallel with the floor. ②

5. Maintain a neutral spine and allow your torso to dip forward slightly.

6. Exhale and push through your heels to extend your legs and return to the starting position.

7. Repeat for the specified number of repetitions.

Kayla's Tip
Think about sitting back on a chair.

SUMO SQUAT
BODY AREA: LOWER BODY

1. Stand with your feet further than shoulder-width apart and your feet pointed slightly outward. This is your starting position. ①

2. Inhale and look straight ahead.

3. Bend at both the hips and knees to lower into a squat, ensuring that your knees remain in line with your toes.

4. Continue bending your knees, aiming to have your upper legs parallel with the floor. ②

5. Keep your back within 45 to 90 degrees of your hips.

6. Exhale and push through your heels to extend your legs and return to the starting position.

7. Repeat for the specified number of repetitions.

Kayla's Tip
The key to this exercise is not letting your knees cave in towards each other. Continue to push them out throughout the movement.

DOUBLE PULSE SQUAT
BODY AREA: LOWER BODY

1. Stand with your feet shoulder-width apart. This is your starting position.

2. Inhale and look straight ahead.

3. Bend at both the hips and knees to lower into a squat, ensuring that your knees remain in line with your toes. ②

4. Continue bending your knees, aiming to have your upper legs parallel with the floor. Maintain a neutral spine and allow your torso to dip forward slightly.

5. Push through your heels and extend your legs slightly, but not all the way back up. ③

6. Bend your knees to return to full squat position.

7. Exhale and push through your heels to extend your legs and return to the starting position.

8. Repeat for the specified number of repetitions.

Kayla's Tip
Keep your knees out and perform each pulse with control.

DOUBLE PULSE SUMO SQUAT
BODY AREA: LOWER BODY

1. Stand with your feet wider than shoulder-width apart, with your feet pointed slightly outward. This is your starting position. ①

2. Inhale and look straight ahead.

3. Bend at both the hips and knees to lower into a squat, ensuring that your knees remain in line with your toes. ②

4. Continue bending your knees, aiming to have your upper legs parallel with the floor.

5. Maintain a neutral spine and allow your torso to dip forward slightly.

6. Push through your heels and extend your legs slightly, but not all the way back up. ③

7. Bend your knees to return to full squat position.

8. Exhale and push through your heels to extend your legs, returning to the starting position.

9. Repeat for the specified number of repetitions or time.

Kayla's Tip
Keep your toes pointed out, knees over toes and pulse with control.

SQUAT TO CALF RAISE
BODY AREA: LOWER BODY

1. Begin standing with your feet shoulder-width apart.

2. Inhale, and looking straight ahead, bend at both the hips and knees to lower into a squat, ensuring that your knees remain in line with your toes. ①

3. Continue bending your knees, aiming to have your upper legs parallel to the floor.

4. Ensure that your back remains between a 45- to 90-degree angle to your hips.

5. Exhale, push through the heels of your feet and extend your knees to return to stand tall.

6. Press into the balls of your feet to raise your heels off the ground. ②

7. Inhale as you lower your heels to return to the starting position.

8. Repeat for the specified number of repetitions or time.

Kayla's Tip
If you feel wobbly during the calf raise, you can hold a chair for balance.

DUMBBELL GOBLET SQUAT
BODY AREA: LOWER BODY

1. Holding a dumbbell with both hands directly in front of your chest, stand with your feet slightly further than shoulder-width apart. This is your starting position. ①

2. Inhale, and while looking straight ahead, bend at both the hips and knees to lower into a squat, ensuring that your knees point toward your toes. ②

3. Continue bending your knees, aiming to have your upper legs parallel with the floor. Maintain a neutral spine and allow your torso to dip forward slightly.

4. Exhale, push through your heels and extend your knees to return to the starting position.

5. Repeat for the specified number of repetitions.

Kayla's Tip
Keep the dumbbell close to your body.

DUMBBELL FRONT SQUAT
BODY AREA: LOWER BODY

1. Begin standing with your feet slightly further than shoulder-width apart, holding a dumbbell in each hand at shoulder height. Point both feet slightly outward. This is your starting position. ①

2. Inhale and engage your core. Looking straight ahead, bend at both the hips and knees to lower into a squat, aiming to have your upper legs parallel with the floor. ②

3. Maintain a neutral spine and allow your torso to dip forward slightly, keeping your knees aligned with your toes.

4. Exhale and push through your heels, extending your legs to return to the starting position.

5. Repeat for the specified number of repetitions or time.

EXERCISES

Kayla's Tip
Keep the dumbbells as close to your body as possible.

STATIC LUNGE
BODY AREA: LOWER BODY

1. Begin standing with your feet in a split stance with your right leg forward and your left leg back, ensuring that your feet are shoulder-width apart. This is your starting position. ❶

2. Inhale as you bend both knees to approximately 90 degrees. Ensure that your front knee is aligned with your ankle and your back knee is hovering just off the floor. ❷

3. Exhale as you extend both knees to return to the starting position.

4. Repeat for the specified number of repetitions on each side.

Kayla's Tip

Think about lunging on train tracks rather than a tightrope, so you have a wide and stable base.

FRONT LUNGE
BODY AREA: LOWER BODY

1. Begin standing with your feet shoulder-width apart. This is your starting position. ①

2. Inhale and carefully take a big step forward with your left foot. Plant your left foot on the floor. ②

3. Bend both knees to approximately 90 degrees, ensuring that your weight is evenly distributed between both legs. Your front knee should be aligned with your ankle and your back knee should be hovering just off the floor. ③

4. Exhale as you extend both knees, transfer your weight completely onto your right foot and step your left foot backward to return to the starting position.

5. Inhale as you carefully take a big step forward with your right foot. Plant your right foot on the floor.

6. Bend both knees to approximately 90 degrees, ensuring that your weight is evenly distributed between both legs. Your front knee should be aligned with your ankle and your back knee should be hovering just off the floor.

7. Exhale as you extend both knees, transfer your weight completely onto your left foot and step your right foot backward to return to the starting position.

8. Continue alternating between left and right for the specified number of repetitions.

Kayla's Tip
Control the movement and keep your core strong for balance as you step forward.

LATERAL LUNGE
BODY AREA: LOWER BODY

1. Begin standing with your feet shoulder-width apart. This is your starting position.

2. Inhale, and keeping your right foot on the floor, release your left foot and take a big step to your left.

3. As you plant your foot on the floor, bend your left knee, ensuring that your right leg remains straight.

4. Exhale as you extend your left knee and transfer your weight onto your right foot.

5. Step your left foot inwards to return to the starting position.

6. Inhale, and keeping your left foot on the floor, release your right foot and take a big step to your right.

7. As you plant your foot on the floor, bend your right knee, ensuring that your left leg remains straight.

8. Exhale as you extend your right knee and transfer your weight onto your left foot.

9. Step your right foot inwards to return to the starting position.

10. Continue alternating between left and right for the specified number of repetitions.

Kayla's Tip
Focus on pushing your hips back as you bend into the lunge.

REVERSE LUNGE
BODY AREA: LOWER BODY

1. Begin standing with your feet shoulder-width apart. This is your starting position. ①

2. Inhale and carefully take a big step backwards with your left foot. Plant your left foot on the floor.

3. Bend both knees to approximately 90 degrees, ensuring that your weight is evenly distributed between both legs. Your front knee should be aligned with your ankle and your back knee should be hovering just off the floor. ②

4. Exhale as you extend both knees, transfer your weight completely onto your right foot, then step your left foot forward to return to the starting position. ③

5. Inhale and carefully take a big step backwards with your right foot. Plant your right foot on the floor.

6. Bend both knees to approximately 90 degrees, ensuring that your weight is evenly distributed between both legs. Your front knee should be aligned with your ankle and your back knee should be hovering just off the floor.

7. Exhale as you extend both knees, transfer your weight completely onto your left foot and step your right foot forward to return to the starting position.

8. Continue alternating between left and right for the specified number of repetitions.

Kayla's Tip
Don't allow the front knee to cave in.

REVERSE LUNGE AND KNEE
BODY AREA: LOWER BODY

1. Stand with your feet shoulder-width apart. This is your starting position.

2. Inhale and carefully take a big step backwards with your right foot. As you plant your foot on the floor, bend both knees to approximately 90 degrees, ensuring that your weight is evenly distributed between both legs. Your front knee should be aligned with your ankle and your back knee should be hovering just off the floor. ❶

3. Exhale as you extend both knees and transfer your weight onto your left foot. At the same time, elevate your right foot to bring your knee into your chest. ❷

4. Inhale as you lower your right leg to return to the starting position, but without resting your foot on the mat. If you can keep your balance, you want this movement to flow straight from the knee lift into the reverse lunge again.

5. Repeat for the specified number of repetitions on each side.

Kayla's Tip
To keep your balance, think about lunging on train tracks rather than a tightrope. Keep your feet shoulder-width apart!

GLUTE BRIDGE
BODY AREA: LOWER BODY

1. Start by lying flat on your back on a yoga mat.

2. Bend your knees and position your feet firmly on the mat, hip-width apart, and maintain a neutral spine with your arms resting by your sides on the mat. This is your starting position. ①

3. Inhale, and draw your belly button towards your spine to engage your core.

4. Exhale, press your heels into the mat, and squeeze your glutes to raise your hips off the floor until your body forms a straight line from chin to knee, resting on your shoulders. ②

5. Inhale as you lower your pelvis to return to the starting position.

6. Repeat for the specified number of repetitions.

Kayla's Tip
Think about pushing your feet into the floor and squeezing your glutes to avoid using your lower back.

GLUTE BRIDGE AND OPENING
BODY AREA: LOWER BODY

1. Start by lying flat on your back on a yoga mat.

2. Bend your knees and position your feet firmly on the mat, ensuring they are hip-width apart and your spine is in a neutral position.

3. Allow your arms to rest by your sides on the mat. This is your starting position.

4. Inhale, then exhale and as you press your heels into the mat, squeeze your glutes to lift your hips off the floor until your body forms a straight line from chin to knee, resting on your shoulders. ①

5. Inhale, and while keeping your hips raised and glutes engaged, open your knees outwards. ②

6. Draw your knees inwards until they are hip-width apart.

7. Exhale and lower your spine onto the mat, gently and with control, followed by your hips.

8. Repeat for the specified number of repetitions.

Kayla's Tip

Don't allow your hips to drop or your back to arch when opening your knees.

GLUTE BRIDGE WALKOUT
BODY AREA: LOWER BODY

1. Start by lying flat on your back on a yoga mat.

2. Bend your knees and position your feet firmly on the mat, ensuring they are hip-width apart and your spine is neutral.

3. Allow your arms to rest by your sides on the mat. This is your starting position.

4. Exhale and gently draw your belly button towards your spine to engage your core.

5. Press your heels into the mat, squeeze your glutes, and raise your hips off the floor until your body forms a straight line from chin to knee, resting on your shoulders.

6. Inhale, and while keeping your hips as still as possible, extend your right leg to step your right foot out, followed by your left foot, until your feet are hip-width apart. Keep your hips elevated.

7. Exhale, and while keeping your hips as still as possible, bend your right knee to step your right foot in, followed by your left foot, returning to the glute bridge position.

8. Continue alternating between sides as you step out for the specified number of repetitions or time.

Kayla's Tip
Try to keep your hips high throughout the movement without arching your back.

SINGLE-LEG GLUTE BRIDGE
BODY AREA: LOWER BODY

1. Lie flat on your back on a yoga mat.

2. Bend your left knee and position your left foot firmly on the mat.

3. Extend your right leg directly in front of you or towards the ceiling.

4. Ensure your spine is in a neutral position and allow your arms to rest by your sides on the mat. This is your starting position.

5. Inhale and draw your belly button towards your spine to engage your core.

6. Exhale, press your left heel into the mat, squeeze your glutes, and raise your hips off the floor until your body forms a straight line from chin to knee, resting on your shoulders.

7. Inhale as you lower your hips to return to the starting position.

8. Repeat for the specified number of repetitions, then switch to the other side.

Kayla's Tip
Don't arch your back, and try to keep your hips level throughout each rep.

HIP THRUST (CHAIR)

BODY AREA: LOWER BODY

1. Begin seated on the ground with your knees bent, feet on the floor hip-width apart, and a chair or bench placed behind you.

2. With your feet firmly planted on the floor, lean back onto the chair so that it gently presses into your upper back.

3. Place your hands on your hips or behind your head, whichever is most comfortable. This is your starting position. ①

4. Inhale, and as you exhale, press your heels into the mat and squeeze your glutes to drive your hips upwards until your body forms one straight line from shoulders to knees, keeping your chin tucked. ②

5. Inhale as you slowly lower your hips to return to the starting position.

6. Repeat for the specified number of repetitions.

Kayla's Tip

Keep your chin tucked and tuck in your pelvis to avoid arching your lower back.

DOUBLE PULSE HIP THRUST (CHAIR)
BODY AREA: LOWER BODY

1. Start with your back against a chair or bench and your feet flat on the ground, with your knees bent and your heels close to your glutes. 1

2. Engage your core and squeeze your glutes to lift your hips up towards the ceiling, using your glutes to drive the movement. 2

3. Pause at the top of the movement and perform two small pulses by slightly lowering and raising your hips. 3

4. After the double pulse, lower your hips back down towards the ground.

5. Repeat the entire sequence, lifting your hips, performing two pulses, and lowering your hips, for the specified number of repetitions.

Kayla's Tip
Think about keeping your tailbone tucked towards your belly button throughout the movement to avoid arching your lower back.

SPLIT STANCE HIP THRUST (CHAIR)
BODY AREA: LOWER BODY

1. Begin seated on the ground with a chair or bench placed behind you.

2. Keep your knees bent and feet hip-width apart, but staggered slightly so that one foot is resting further out than the other.

3. Lean back onto the chair so that it gently presses into your upper back.

4. Place your hands on your hips or behind your head, whichever is most comfortable. This is your starting position.

5. Inhale, and as you exhale, press your heels into the mat and squeeze your glutes to raise your hips off the floor until your body forms one straight line from shoulders to knees, keeping your chin tucked.

6. Inhale as you slowly lower your hips to return to the starting position.

7. Repeat for the specified number of repetitions, then swap sides.

Kayla's Tip
Make sure the foot that is further out is resting on your heel and your other foot is at a 90-degree angle.

SINGLE-LEG HIP THRUST (CHAIR)
BODY AREA: LOWER BODY

1. Begin seated on the ground with a chair or bench placed behind you, feet hip-width apart, and your knees bent.

2. With your feet firmly planted on the floor, lean back onto the chair so that it gently presses into your upper back.

3. Place your hands on your hips or behind your head, whichever is most comfortable. Slightly lift your left foot off the ground. This is your starting position. ①

4. Inhale, and as you exhale, press your right heel into the mat and squeeze your glutes to lift your hips off the floor until your body forms one straight line from shoulder to knee, keeping your chin tucked. ②

5. Keep your left foot elevated off the ground and held in a position that is comfortable throughout the exercise.

6. Inhale as you slowly lower your hips to return to the starting position.

7. Repeat for the specified number of repetitions or time on each side.

Kayla's Tip
Don't touch the lifted leg to the ground until you've completed all of your reps - make sure to keep it up.

INCLINE PUSH-UP (KNEES, CHAIR)
BODY AREA: UPPER BODY

1. Place a chair or bench in front of you.

2. Place both hands on the seat of the chair slightly further than shoulder-width apart.

3. Position your feet together on the floor behind you, resting on your knees. This is your starting position. 1

4. Inhale, and while maintaining a neutral spine, bend your elbows and lower your torso towards the chair until your arms form two 90-degree angles. 2

5. Exhale, push through your chest and extend your elbows to lift your body back into the starting position.

6. Repeat for the specified number of repetitions.

Kayla's Tip
Keep your elbows close to the sides of your body. Don't allow them to flare high and wide.

PUSH-UP (KNEES)
BODY AREA: UPPER BODY

1. Place both hands on the floor slightly further than shoulder-width apart and both feet together behind you, resting on your knees.

2. Draw your belly button towards your spine to engage your core. This is your starting position. ①

3. Inhale as you bend your elbows and lower your torso towards the floor until your arms form two 90-degree angles. ②

4. Maintain a straight back and an engaged core throughout the movement.

5. Exhale as you push through your chest and extend your arms, lifting your body back into the starting position.

6. Repeat for the specified number of repetitions.

Kayla's Tip
Think about keeping a straight line from your knees to shoulders to ensure your hips lower to the floor, too. They shouldn't be up in the air!

LYING-DOWN PUSH-UP (KNEES)
BODY AREA: UPPER BODY

1. Place both hands on the mat slightly further than shoulder-width apart, resting on your knees and the balls of your feet.

2. Draw your belly button towards your spine to engage your core. This is your starting position. ①

3. Inhale, and while maintaining a neutral spine, bend your elbows and lower your torso to the mat. ②

4. Release your hands and extend both arms out in front of you. ③

5. Bring your arms back in towards your body and place your hands on the mat on either side of your chest. ④

6. Exhale as you push through your chest and extend your elbows to lift your body back into the starting position.

7. Repeat for the specified number of repetitions.

Kayla's Tip
Focus on the pushing up part and breathe out during this.

TRICEP DIP (CHAIR)
BODY AREA: UPPER BODY

1. Begin seated on a chair or bench.

2. Place your hands on the front edge of the chair under your glutes and directly below your shoulders, with your fingers facing forwards.

3. Shift your glutes forwards off the chair. This is your starting position. **1**

4. Inhale as you bend your elbows to lower your glutes towards the floor, ensuring that your shoulders, elbows and wrists remain in line with one another. Think about keeping your elbows close to your body throughout the movement. **2**

5. Once you have reached a 90-degree angle with your arms, exhale and push through the palms of your hands and extend your arms to return to the starting position.

6. Avoid using your legs to assist you and always try to maintain an upright position.

7. Repeat for the specified number of repetitions.

Kayla's Tip
Perform these in a slow and controlled way. Don't bounce up from the bottom.

DUMBBELL CURL AND PRESS
BODY AREA: UPPER BODY

1. Stand with your feet shoulder-width apart, holding a dumbbell in each hand in a neutral grip (palms facing inwards) with arms extended on either side of your body. This is your starting position. ①

2. Inhale as you bend your elbows to bring the dumbbells in towards your chest, ensuring that your elbows remain as close as possible to the sides of your body. ②

3. Exhale as you extend your elbows and press the dumbbells up above your head, ensuring that your arms are in line with your ears on either side of your head. ③

4. Once your arms are fully extended, inhale as you bend your elbows to lower the dumbbells into your chest.

5. Exhale as you extend your elbows to lower the dumbbells in front of your body and return to the starting position.

Kayla's Tip
Don't arch your back as you press overhead.

DUMBBELL BENT-OVER ROW
BODY AREA: UPPER BODY

1. Hold a dumbbell in each hand with a neutral grip (palms facing inwards) and stand with your feet shoulder-width apart.

2. While maintaining a slight bend in your knees, hinge forward from your hips so that your torso is at a 45-degree angle to the floor. Extend your arms directly below your chest. This is your starting position. ❶

3. Inhale, and as you exhale, bend your elbows to bring the dumbbells in towards your body, ensuring your elbows remain close to the sides of your body. You should feel a small squeeze between your shoulder blades. ❷

4. Inhale as you extend your elbows to lower the dumbbells and return to the starting position.

5. Repeat for the specified number of repetitions.

Kayla's Tip
Think about your elbows sweeping past your hips.

MODIFIED AB BIKE
BODY AREA: CORE

1. Begin lying face-up on a yoga mat, with your feet on the floor and hands behind your ears. Inhale and draw your belly button towards your spine to engage your core. This is your starting position.

2. Exhale, and while engaging through your abdominals, release your right foot off the floor and draw your knee in towards you. At the same time, raise and twist your torso to bring your left elbow towards your right knee. You should feel tension in your abdominals throughout the movement. ②

3. Inhale and lower your leg and arm to return to the starting position.

4. Alternate between sides for the specified number of repetitions or time. ③

Kayla's Tip
Perform these in a slow and controlled way, feeling your core engaged and keeping your back on the floor.

AB BIKES
BODY AREA: CORE

1. Start by lying on your back on a yoga mat with your legs extended out in front of you.

2. Bend your elbows and place your hands behind your earlobes.

3. Gently raise both legs and your head and shoulders off the mat. This is your starting position.

4. While keeping your right leg extended, bend your left knee and draw it in towards your chest.

5. At the same time, rotate your torso to the left to bring your right elbow to your knee.

6. Untwist your torso and extend your left knee to return to the starting position.

7. Immediately bend your right knee and draw it in towards your chest as you rotate your torso to the right to bring your left elbow to your knee.

8. Untwist your torso and extend your right knee to return to the starting position.

9. Alternate between left and right for the specified number of repetitions, continuing to breathe throughout.

Kayla's Tip
Keep your hands behind your ears and your core engaged. Push your foot out as if you are pushing something away.

SINGLE-ARM AND LEG JACKKNIFE
BODY AREA: CORE

1. Start by lying on your back on a yoga mat with your hands placed behind your ears. This is your starting position. ①

2. Inhale and engage your core.

3. Exhale as you simultaneously raise your left leg and right hand off the floor to meet in the middle.

4. Slowly lift your head, shoulder blades and torso off the floor, ensuring that your left shoulder remains pressed into the mat. ②

5. Return to the starting position without resting your head back on the floor to maintain tension throughout your core.

6. Repeat for the specified number of repetitions or time on each side.

Kayla's Tip
Keeping your head off the floor will help you get the most out of this exercise and avoid neck pain.

AB BIKE TO JACKKNIFE
BODY AREA: CORE

1. Start by lying on your back on a yoga mat with your legs on the floor straight out in front of you and slightly bent. Bend your elbows and place your hands behind your earlobes. Gently raise both legs, your head and shoulders off the mat. This is your starting position. ①

2. Inhale, and while keeping your right leg extended, bend your left knee and draw it in towards your chest. At the same time, rotate your torso to the left to bring your right elbow to your knee. ②

3. Untwist your torso and extend your left leg to return to the starting position. ③

4. Exhale as you immediately elevate your left leg so that it is at a 90-degree angle to your hips. At the same time, extend your right arm to bring your hand up towards your left foot – slowly lifting your head, shoulder blades and torso off the mat. ④

5. Inhale as you lower your torso, shoulder blades and head to the mat. Lower your left leg and place your right hand behind your earlobes to return to the starting position.

6. Complete half of the specified number of repetitions on the same side before completing the remaining repetitions on the other side.

Kayla's Tip
Make sure to rotate your torso but try to keep your spine on the floor to avoid arching your back.

PLANK (KNEES)
BODY AREA: CORE

1. Start by placing your forearms (wrist to elbow) firmly on the mat, ensuring that your elbows are directly below your shoulders.

2. Extend both legs behind you and rest on your knees, elevating your hips off the mat.

3. Brace your abdominals and ensure that your spine remains in a neutral position.

4. Hold this position for the specified amount of time, breathing deeply throughout.

Kayla's Tip
Keep a straight line from shoulders to knees – don't allow your hips to sag down or rise up.

PLANK (TOES)
BODY AREA: CORE

1. Start by placing your forearms (wrist to elbow) firmly on the mat, ensuring that your elbows are directly below your shoulders.

2. Extend both legs behind you and rest on the balls of your feet.

3. Engage your core and lift your hips off the mat, forming a straight line from your head to your heels with your spine in a neutral position.

4. Hold this position for the specified amount of time, breathing deeply throughout.

Kayla's Tip
The longer you go, the harder it is.

PLANK AND SHOULDER TAP (KNEES)
BODY AREA: CORE

1. Place both hands on the mat slightly further than shoulder-width apart, with feet together on the mat behind you while resting on your knees.

2. Draw your belly button towards your spine to engage your core. This is your starting position. ①

3. While maintaining a neutral spine, release your right hand and reach across your body to touch your left shoulder. ②

4. Ensure that you brace your abdominals to keep your hips parallel to the floor.

5. Lower your right hand to return to the starting position.

6. Alternate between lifting your right and left hand for the specified number of repetitions or time. Think about pushing away from the ground with your hand to keep your upper body elevated, and maintain control of your breathing throughout the movement. ③

Kayla's Tip
Don't let your torso rotate side to side. Keep your core nice and strong and your hips level.

HIGH PLANK AND SHOULDER TAP
BODY AREA: CORE

1. Place both hands on the mat slightly further than shoulder-width apart, feet apart on the mat behind you while resting on the balls of your feet. This is your starting position. ①

2. Release your right hand and reach across your body to touch your left shoulder, keeping your core engaged and your hips parallel to the floor. ②

3. Lower your right hand to return to the starting position. ③

4. Release your left hand and reach across your body to touch your right shoulder, once again keeping your core engaged and your hips parallel to the floor. ④

5. Lower your left hand to return to the starting position.

6. Continue alternating between right and left for the specified amount of time, inhaling for two repetitions and exhaling for two repetitions.

Kayla's Tip
Try to remain as steady as possible and avoid letting your hips rotate.

SIDE PLANK
BODY AREA: CORE

1. Start by lying on your right side lengthways along a yoga mat, with your legs stacked on top of one another.

2. Place your right forearm firmly on the floor, ensuring that your elbow is directly below your shoulder and your forearm is parallel to the short edge of your mat.

3. Keep your knees together and bend your bottom knee to a 90-degree angle, so that one leg is bent behind you.

4. Draw your belly button towards your spine to engage your core.

5. Using your obliques, raise your hips off the mat, maintaining a straight line from head to knee. ①

6. Hold this position for half of the specified amount of time, and then switch to the other side to complete the remaining time.

Kayla's Tip
Remain in a straight line from shoulder to knee. For a challenge, keep both feet together rather than bending one leg.

SIDE PLANK AND HIP DIP
BODY AREA: CORE

1. Start by lying on your right side lengthways along a yoga mat, with your legs stacked on top of one another. Place your right forearm firmly on the floor, ensuring that your elbow is directly below your shoulder and that your forearm is parallel to the short edge of your mat.

2. Keep your knees together and bend your bottom knee to a 90-degree angle, so that one leg is bent behind you. This is your starting position.

3. Inhale and engage your core.

4. Exhale as you use your obliques to lift your hips off the floor. ❶

5. Lower your hips slightly, then elevate them again. ❷

6. Repeat for the specified number of repetitions on each side.

Kayla's Tip

Take these in a slow and controlled way, so you can feel your core control the movement.

STANDING X CRUNCH
BODY AREA: CORE

1. Begin standing with your feet shoulder-width apart.

2. Place both hands behind your head. Draw your belly button towards your spine to engage your core. This is your starting position. ①

3. While keeping your right leg extended, bend your left knee and draw it in towards your chest. ②

4. At the same time, rotate your torso to the left to bring your right elbow to your knee.

5. Untwist your torso and extend your left knee to return to the starting position. ③

6. Immediately bend your right knee and draw it in towards your chest.

7. Rotate your torso to the right to bring your left elbow to your knee. ④

8. Untwist your torso and extend your right knee to return to the starting position.

9. Continue alternating between sides for the specified number of repetitions or time. Maintain control of your breathing throughout the exercise.

Kayla's Tip
Perform these with a bit of speed to add a cardio element, or move slowly and with control to feel the burn.

MODIFIED WALKOUT BURPEE (CHAIR)
BODY AREA: FULL BODY

1. Place a chair or bench in front of you with the seat facing towards you.

2. Stand one step away from the chair with your feet shoulder-width apart. This is your starting position.

3. Bend at both the hips and knees as you place your hands on the chair. ①

4. Inhale and draw your belly button towards your spine to engage your core while ensuring your spine remains in a neutral position.

5. Step your feet backwards, one at a time, so that your legs are completely extended behind you, resting on the balls of your feet. Your body should be in one straight line from your head to your heels, in a high plank position. ② ③

6. Step both of your feet forwards, one at a time, ensuring that your feet remain shoulder-width apart. ④ ⑤

7. Exhale as you extend your legs, stand up tall and reach your arms above your head.

8. As you reach the top of your stance, press into the balls of your feet to raise your heels off the ground. ⑥

9. Inhale as you lower your arms and heels to return to the starting position.

10. Repeat for the specified number of repetitions.

Kayla's Tip
Slow it down at the start and build in some speed once you have mastered the movement.

SQUAT AND HIGH REACH
BODY AREA: FULL BODY

1. Begin standing with your feet slightly further than shoulder-width apart, hands by your side.

2. Draw your belly button towards your spine to engage your core. This is your starting position.

3. Inhale as you bend at both the hips and knees, aiming to have your upper legs parallel with the floor. ①

4. Ensure you keep a proud chest and that your knees remain in line with your toes (don't allow your knees to fall in).

5. Exhale and push evenly through your feet to extend your legs and stand up tall.

6. As you reach the top of your stance, press into the balls of your feet to raise your heels off the ground.

7. At the same time, extend your arms directly overhead, keeping your arms close to your ears. ②

8. Repeat for the specified number of repetitions or time.

Kayla's Tip
You can perform these with a bit of speed to add a cardio element.

LATERAL LUNGE TO KNEE UP
BODY AREA: FULL BODY

1. Stand with your feet shoulder-width apart. This is your starting position.

2. Keeping your right foot on the floor, release your left foot and take a big step to your left. As you plant your foot on the floor, bend your left knee, ensuring that your right leg remains straight. ①

3. Extend your left knee and transfer your weight onto your right foot. Just as your weight returns to centre, lift your left knee up and across your body to crunch and touch your right elbow. ②

4. Repeat for the specified number of repetitions on each side.

EXERCISES

Kayla's Tip
Take it slow to start and maintain your balance.

WEEK 1
MINDSET

KAYLA'S PEP TALK:
MINDSET

Hitting reboot on your health and fitness journey can happen at any stage of life, but in my experience, I've found that it's often spurred on by a desire for change. Perhaps you've been feeling far from your best, your current routine has lost its shine, other priorities have gotten in the way lately, or you simply know in your gut that it's about time you put yourself first.

But there's a tough, yet important, pill to swallow when it comes to making any kind of lifestyle change. Unless you're also taking the time to get the *inside* right and work on your mindset, any change you make isn't going to feel anywhere near as good as you want it to. Give yourself a huge advantage by getting your head in the right place.

Ultimately, I want you to start day one of your reboot feeling empowered and positive within yourself – so no matter what progress you make, what setbacks you face, or how your fitness journey evolves throughout (and beyond) these four weeks, you've always got that undercurrent of empowerment and positivity motivating you.

After the birth of each of my children, Arna and Jax, my body couldn't do what it used to. Over the years, I've had shingles, pneumonia and surgery for endometriosis. There have been moments of turning the treadmill off after a few minutes, struggling through a single push-up, feeling lost and battling through illness, but throughout every challenge and setback I've faced, I never felt like it was me *against* my body.

You might have heard the expression 'It's you against you' before – it's often thrown around as a pep talk to encourage people not to compare themselves to others. But I want you to be on your own team. I want your biggest supporter to be in your own head.

If your headspace and your relationship with fitness feel far from positive right now, you can start to shift your mindset by looking for the good and finding things to be thankful for.

You might not be exactly where you want to be, but you can be grateful for making the decision to begin, and for the exciting journey that lies ahead.

You might not feel your best every day, but you can be grateful for still showing up, for your body, for the loved ones supporting you, and for the little wins that remind you just how far you've come.

You might feel like you're not making any progress towards your goals until you realise how grateful you are for every mind-clearing walk, every good night's sleep, every endorphin rush, and the unbeatable feeling you get from accomplishing something you couldn't do before.

You might have previously felt that working out and nourishing your body was a chore. Maybe this is the time you rewire that perspective. Moving your body, eating well and putting yourself first isn't something you *have* to do, it's something you *get* to do.

Setting yourself up for a fitness journey that feels empowering and positive also means getting clear on your why, and making sure it's both inspiring and unique to you.

Maybe you think the why behind your reboot is to be fit and healthy. Let's dig a little deeper. What's underneath that? Find what it is that will *really* keep you going. Is it to reduce your risk of illness? Feel confident in your skin? See what you're really capable of? Step into the best version of you? The more personal, honest and emotive your why feels, the better.

Imagine getting up in the morning and being the most confident version of yourself. You can walk into the gym with ease and build on your progress. Imagine being able to run, lift or move your body in a way that you can't right now. Imagine having so much to do, but knowing you've got more than enough energy to get it done. Imagine the *ultimate* you.

Empowering your mind also means learning to push yourself and hold yourself accountable, minus the self-criticism. As women, we are so critical of ourselves, and I want your reboot experience to silence those voices rather than amplify them. Negative self-talk isn't helpful or kind, and that critical voice will still be there even once you've achieved your goals. So kick it to the curb from day one and speak to yourself like you would to your best friend.

You've got this. Keep going. Just one more rep. You're worth the effort. One day at a time. You're doing an amazing job. Don't give up. You know you can do it.

Some weeks you'll achieve incredible things, other weeks you'll be dealing with setbacks. Some days you'll feel on top of the world, other days will feel like a slog. Throughout all of it, I've got your back – and I want you to be backing yourself every step of the way, too.

Be grateful for everything your body and mind can do.

WEEK 1 KEY: GRATITUDE

I don't just want to empower you to make fitness a habit, but to help you feel your very best, inside and out. And part of that is helping you to feel a sense of gratitude for everything your body and mind are capable of.

Practising gratitude and actively changing the language you use to speak to yourself is an incredible way to transform how you feel about your body. It's also a great tool to have up your sleeve on those days you're feeling anxious or stressed. In those moments when you're struck by feelings of self-doubt, gratitude can help you reset.

This week, where we're starting with mindset, I want you to focus on how fitness can be an act of self-empowerment, a way to break through your self-prescribed limits, to reinvent yourself and realise you're capable of so much more than you ever thought possible. Moving your body unlocks so many opportunities to feel good and see the good – in yourself and in every aspect of your life.

An incredible way to harness the power of positive self-talk when it comes to fitness is through a regular gratitude practice. These workouts aren't a punishment or a space in which you should criticise yourself – they're about feeling good within and about yourself.

Use these pages to celebrate everything you're capable of or start to rewrite the narrative of your journey. From here on, think of each session as something you are lucky enough to do. These workouts are a way to honour where you're at today and move closer to the best version of you.

This week, I want you to find the time to write down five things you're grateful to your body for. Perhaps it's for growing your children. Or holding your plank for that extra 10 seconds. Or being a safe shoulder for a friend to cry on.

Your most important relationship is the one you have with yourself. Be grateful for it. Honour it. Nourish it. Protect it. Prioritise acts of self-care and self-compassion. Make time for the things that fill your cup. Love yourself just as much as you do everyone around you. And as exciting as it is to step into the best version of you, never forget: you are already incredible in so many ways. Inside *and* out.

WEEK 1 MEAL PLANNER

Tip: Have a shopping list handy while you record your plans.

MONDAY

BREAKFAST

SNACK

LUNCH

SNACK

DINNER

TUESDAY

B

S

L

S

D

WEDNESDAY

B

S

L

S

D

THURSDAY

B

S

L

S

D

FRIDAY

B

S

L

S

D

SATURDAY

B

S

L

S

D

SUNDAY

B

S

L

S

D

WEEK 1 MOVEMENT PLAN

WEEKLY GOAL: Complete any 2 sessions
EQUIPMENT: None

SESSION 1
WALK

EXERCISE	REPS/TIME
Walk, treadmill or outdoor	20 minutes

SESSION 2
MOBILITY
CIRCUIT

EXERCISE	REPS/TIME	LAPS
Cat-cow (page 96)	30 seconds	2
Four-point thoracic rotation (page 98)	16 reps (8 per side)	
Child's pose (page 93)	30 seconds	
Tricep stretch (page 95)	40 seconds (20 per side)	

SESSION 3
STRENGTH
WORKOUT 1
CIRCUIT

EXERCISE	REPS/TIME	LAPS
Squat (page 101)	10 reps	3
Glute bridge (page 113)	10 reps	
Incline push-up (knees, chair) (page 121)	6 reps	
Rest	30 seconds	

SESSION 4
STRENGTH
WORKOUT 2
CIRCUIT

EXERCISE	REPS/TIME	LAPS
Static lunge (page 108)	16 reps (8 per side)	3
Sit squat (chair) (page 100)	10 reps	
Hip thrust (chair) (page 117)	10 reps	
Rest	30 seconds	

WEEK 1: DAY 1

Date: /   /

HOW AM I FEELING TODAY?

_____

_____

_____

I AM GRATEFUL FOR:

_____

_____

_____

MOVEMENT GOAL:

_____

SOMETHING I WANT TO ACHIEVE TODAY:

_____

_____

_____

EVENING CHECK-IN

MOVEMENT GOAL COMPLETED ◯

WATER _____

WHAT AM I PROUD OF TODAY?

WHEN I MOVED MY BODY, I FELT:

_____   _____

_____   _____

_____   _____

WHAT AM I LOOKING FORWARD TO TOMORROW?

_____

_____

_____

WEEK 1: DAY 2

Date: /   /

HOW AM I FEELING TODAY?

_____

_____

_____

I AM GRATEFUL FOR:

_____

_____

_____

MOVEMENT GOAL:

_____

SOMETHING I WANT TO ACHIEVE TODAY:

_____

_____

_____

EVENING CHECK-IN

MOVEMENT GOAL COMPLETED ◯

WATER _____

WHAT AM I PROUD OF TODAY?

WHEN I MOVED MY BODY, I FELT:

_____   _____

_____   _____

_____

WHAT AM I LOOKING FORWARD TO TOMORROW?

_____

_____

_____

WEEK 1: DAY 3

Date: /   /

HOW AM I FEELING TODAY?

_____
_____
_____

I AM GRATEFUL FOR:

_____
_____
_____

MOVEMENT GOAL:

_____

SOMETHING I WANT TO ACHIEVE TODAY:

_____
_____
_____

EVENING CHECK-IN

MOVEMENT GOAL COMPLETED ◯

WATER _____

WHAT AM I PROUD OF TODAY?

_____   WHEN I MOVED MY BODY, I FELT:

_____   _____
_____   _____
_____

WHAT AM I LOOKING FORWARD TO TOMORROW?

_____
_____
_____

152

WEEK 1: DAY 4

Date: / /

HOW AM I FEELING TODAY?

_____

_____

_____

I AM GRATEFUL FOR:

_____

_____

_____

MOVEMENT GOAL:

_____

SOMETHING I WANT TO ACHIEVE TODAY:

_____

_____

EVENING CHECK-IN

MOVEMENT GOAL COMPLETED ◯

WATER _____

WHAT AM I PROUD OF TODAY?

WHEN I MOVED MY BODY, I FELT:

_____

_____

_____

WHAT AM I LOOKING FORWARD TO TOMORROW?

_____

_____

_____

It's never
too late to be
the person
you want
to be.

WEEK 1: DAY 5

Date: / /

HOW AM I FEELING TODAY?

_____
_____
_____

I AM GRATEFUL FOR:

_____
_____
_____

MOVEMENT GOAL:

_____

SOMETHING I WANT TO ACHIEVE TODAY:

_____
_____
_____

EVENING CHECK-IN

MOVEMENT GOAL COMPLETED ◯

WATER _____

WHAT AM I PROUD OF TODAY?

_____
_____
_____

WHEN I MOVED MY BODY, I FELT:

_____
_____
_____

WHAT AM I LOOKING FORWARD TO TOMORROW?

_____
_____
_____

WEEK 1: DAY 6

Date: /   /

HOW AM I FEELING TODAY?

_____

_____

_____

I AM GRATEFUL FOR:

_____

_____

_____

MOVEMENT GOAL:

_____

SOMETHING I WANT TO ACHIEVE TODAY:

_____

_____

_____

EVENING CHECK-IN

MOVEMENT GOAL COMPLETED   ◯

WATER _____

WHAT AM I PROUD OF TODAY?

WHEN I MOVED MY BODY, I FELT:

_____   _____

_____   _____

_____   _____

WHAT AM I LOOKING FORWARD TO TOMORROW?

_____

_____

_____

WEEK 1: DAY 7

Date: /   /

HOW AM I FEELING TODAY?

_____

_____

_____

I AM GRATEFUL FOR:

_____

_____

_____

MOVEMENT GOAL:

_____

SOMETHING I WANT TO ACHIEVE TODAY:

_____

_____

_____

EVENING CHECK-IN

MOVEMENT GOAL COMPLETED ◯

WATER _____

WHAT AM I PROUD OF TODAY?

WHEN I MOVED MY BODY, I FELT:

_____   _____

_____   _____

_____

WHAT AM I LOOKING FORWARD TO TOMORROW?

_____

_____

_____

WEEK 2
MOVEMENT

KAYLA'S PEP TALK:
MOVEMENT

Movement makes me a better me. The *best* me. And after years of training women in my backyard, in gyms, and around the world at boot camps and through the Sweat app, I can make a pretty good guess that movement will make you a better you, too.

I don't just mean 'better' in the sense of getting fitter or stronger (although those perks are massive), but movement can help you feel better *inside*, too. Regular movement can improve your resilience, confidence, outlook, patience and determination.

I love to nourish my body with movement in so many ways. My daily walks are a chance to enjoy watching a show while on my treadmill, an opportunity to get outside and clear my head, or even just hang out with my dogs. Lifting weights builds my physical and mental strength for whatever might be thrown at me. HIIT workouts with fast music make me feel energised. Stretching and foam rolling are ways to tune in to and become far better at listening to my body and what it needs.

And bringing the same level of commitment to my workouts that I bring to a business meeting or a family dinner is a way to show myself and my loved ones where my values lie – that prioritising my wellbeing matters.

I'm sure you already know many of the health benefits of a consistent fitness routine – better cognitive function, sleep, body composition, bone and muscular strength, heart health and mobility, to name a few – but one of my favourite benefits of movement is how it can elevate you as a person.

Suddenly, you're able to walk into a room with a new sense of confidence, your energy is brighter and people comment on how happy you look. You're too busy trying to achieve your health and fitness goals to even think about sweating the small stuff any more, and your idea of what you thought was possible for yourself and your life begins to expand.

You start to think: *If I'm capable of doing this, what else can I do?*

I've seen movement be what drives women to forge stronger relationships and new career pathways, discover their place within a community, experience mental and physical health breakthroughs, or close the door on parts of their life that are no longer serving them.

Moving your body is such a simple way to feel better within yourself. And the better you feel, the more you'll want to build a life that reflects your new energy.

At the end of your four-week reboot, I don't just want you to be able to say that you completed a bunch of workouts, hit your daily step target most days or that your fitness has improved. And I definitely don't want your fourth week training with me to be the end of your journey.

When you challenge yourself with your workouts and start to level up your fitness, you begin to realise what your body is capable of and how much better it feels to be fit and healthy. I want you to get to the point where you don't want to stop – where going back to how things were before, and how *you* were before, just isn't an option.

The shape that movement takes in your own life will be unique to you, your body and your lifestyle. So have some fun experimenting – with different styles of movement, equipment, workout buddies, training times, locations or even clothes! See what lights you up the most and what feels like the best fit for your life.

For me, HIIT has always been what makes me feel in my element. For you, it might be a mix of HIIT and heavy lifting, or weights and walking, or boxing and barre. Perhaps you wake up each day craving a morning workout, or love winding down each day with a gentle yoga flow. Even once you've found a routine you love, it'll still be tough at times, but you'll keep at it when you know how worthwhile it is.

As you power through each workout, plug your headphones in for each walk or roll out your mat for each stretch session, don't think about how many days you've got left. Instead, think about how, with every passing day (even when it feels like a grind), the active habits you're trying to build are feeling more and more like second nature.

Let every Sweat session this week be an opportunity to release what's holding you down and unleash what you've been holding back.

From here on, every move you make means taking another step towards the best version of you.

One foot in front
of the other.

WEEK 2 KEY: WALKING

Throughout your fitness journey, there are going to be weeks when you're absolutely loving it and knocking every session out of the park, and then there will also be times when you can't even be bothered lacing up your sneakers.

I still have days where I just sit in my car outside the gym, trying to figure out how to muster up enough energy to walk in the door. Each week, no matter how your training is going, I want you to keep focusing on just putting one foot in front of the other. Literally.

I can't talk enough about the benefits of walking and it's something I hope to be doing with ease for the rest of my life. It's always been an important part of my routine, whether it's our morning stroll to grab a coffee or at home on the treadmill on a rainy day, and it has *always* been a key part of my workout programs.

The benefits of walking go far beyond improving fitness and include everything from strengthening your bones, muscles and immune system, to helping to prevent or manage various conditions such as heart disease and stroke.[1]

Walking might not feel as intense as a sweaty HIIT workout, but exercise doesn't have to be intense to be worth your time! Walking is still an amazing way to boost your cardiovascular fitness and sleep quality. It can also help boost blood flow and help your body recover between workouts!

Recently, I was talking to a woman in the Sweat Community about her goals, and her reason to stay active was to be as healthy and independent as possible, for as long as possible. I *love* that.

People often assume that walking is for beginners or people who can't run – and it's *just not true*. Walking is not only an underrated form of exercise, but an incredible way to clear your mind, spend time with friends and family or have some much-needed me time.

As you focus on moving your body more this week, try to make walking a key part of that. Depending on your fitness level and schedule, this could mean setting a daily step goal, going for a 30-minute walk several times a week, or adding more walking breaks into your work day. During your reboot journey, I want you to focus on becoming an active person, not *just* with your workouts, but throughout your entire life.

WEEK 2 MEAL PLANNER

Tip: Have a shopping list handy while you record your plans.

MONDAY

BREAKFAST

SNACK

LUNCH

SNACK

DINNER

TUESDAY

B

S

L

S

D

WEDNESDAY

B

S

L

S

D

THURSDAY

B

S

L

S

D

FRIDAY

B

S

L

S

D

SATURDAY

B

S

L

S

D

SUNDAY

B

S

L

S

D

WEEK 2 MOVEMENT PLAN

WEEKLY GOAL: Complete any 2 sessions
EQUIPMENT: None

SESSION 1
WALK

EXERCISE	REPS/TIME
Walk, treadmill or outdoor	25 minutes

SESSION 2
MOBILITY
CIRCUIT

EXERCISE	REPS/TIME	LAPS
Piriformis stretch (chair) (page 88)	60 seconds (30 per side)	2
Neck stretch (chair) (page 94)	40 seconds (20 per side)	
90/90 wipers (page 90)	60 seconds	
Hip flexor stretch (page 87)	60 seconds (30 per side)	

SESSION 3
STRENGTH
WORKOUT 1
CIRCUIT

EXERCISE	REPS/TIME	LAPS
Sumo squat (page 102)	12 reps	3
Glute bridge walkout (page 115)	12 reps	
Push-up (knees) (page 122)	20 reps	
Modified ab bike (page 127)	30 seconds	
Rest	30 seconds	

SESSION 4
STRENGTH
WORKOUT 2
CIRCUIT

EXERCISE	REPS/TIME	LAPS
Reverse lunge (page 111)	20 reps (10 per side)	3
Squat to calf raise (page 105)	12 reps	
Double-pulse hip thrust (chair) (page 118)	12 reps	
Plank (knees) (page 131)	40 seconds	
Rest	30 seconds	

WEEK 2: DAY 1

Date: /   /

HOW AM I FEELING TODAY?

_____

_____

_____

I AM GRATEFUL FOR:

_____

_____

_____

MOVEMENT GOAL:

_____

SOMETHING I WANT TO ACHIEVE TODAY:

_____

_____

_____

EVENING CHECK-IN

MOVEMENT GOAL COMPLETED ◯

WATER _____

WHAT AM I PROUD OF TODAY?

WHEN I MOVED MY BODY, I FELT:

_____

_____

_____

_____

WHAT AM I LOOKING FORWARD TO TOMORROW?

_____

_____

_____

WEEK 2: DAY 2

Date: /   /

HOW AM I FEELING TODAY?

_____
_____
_____

I AM GRATEFUL FOR:

_____
_____
_____

MOVEMENT GOAL:

_____

SOMETHING I WANT TO ACHIEVE TODAY:

_____
_____

EVENING CHECK-IN

MOVEMENT GOAL COMPLETED ◯

WATER _____

WHAT AM I PROUD OF TODAY?

WHEN I MOVED MY BODY, I FELT:

_____   _____
_____   _____

WHAT AM I LOOKING FORWARD TO TOMORROW?

_____
_____
_____

WEEK 2: DAY 3

Date: / /

HOW AM I FEELING TODAY?

_____
_____
_____

I AM GRATEFUL FOR:

_____
_____
_____

MOVEMENT GOAL:

_____

SOMETHING I WANT TO ACHIEVE TODAY:

_____
_____
_____

EVENING CHECK-IN

MOVEMENT GOAL COMPLETED ◯

WATER _____

WHAT AM I PROUD OF TODAY?

_____
_____
_____

WHEN I MOVED MY BODY, I FELT:

_____
_____
_____

WHAT AM I LOOKING FORWARD TO TOMORROW?

_____
_____
_____

WEEK 2: DAY 4

Date: /   /

HOW AM I FEELING TODAY?

_____
_____
_____

I AM GRATEFUL FOR:

_____
_____
_____

MOVEMENT GOAL:

_____

SOMETHING I WANT TO ACHIEVE TODAY:

_____
_____
_____

EVENING CHECK-IN

MOVEMENT GOAL COMPLETED ◯

WATER _____

WHAT AM I PROUD OF TODAY?

_____
_____
_____

WHEN I MOVED MY BODY, I FELT:

_____
_____
_____

WHAT AM I LOOKING FORWARD TO TOMORROW?

_____
_____
_____

What seems
impossible
today
will one day
become your
warm-up.

WEEK 2: DAY 5

Date: /   /

HOW AM I FEELING TODAY?

_____
_____
_____

I AM GRATEFUL FOR:

_____
_____
_____

MOVEMENT GOAL:

_____

SOMETHING I WANT TO ACHIEVE TODAY:

_____
_____

EVENING CHECK-IN

MOVEMENT GOAL COMPLETED ◯

WATER _____

WHAT AM I PROUD OF TODAY?

WHEN I MOVED MY BODY, I FELT:

_____   _____
_____   _____

WHAT AM I LOOKING FORWARD TO TOMORROW?

_____
_____
_____

WEEK 2: DAY 6

Date: / /

HOW AM I FEELING TODAY?

_____

_____

_____

I AM GRATEFUL FOR:

_____

_____

_____

MOVEMENT GOAL:

_____

SOMETHING I WANT TO ACHIEVE TODAY:

_____

_____

_____

EVENING CHECK-IN

MOVEMENT GOAL COMPLETED ◯

WATER _____

WHAT AM I PROUD OF TODAY?

WHEN I MOVED MY BODY, I FELT:

_____   _____

_____   _____

_____   _____

WHAT AM I LOOKING FORWARD TO TOMORROW?

_____

_____

_____

WEEK 2: DAY 7

HOW AM I FEELING TODAY?

_____
_____
_____

I AM GRATEFUL FOR:

_____
_____
_____

MOVEMENT GOAL:

_____

SOMETHING I WANT TO ACHIEVE TODAY:

_____
_____
_____

EVENING CHECK-IN

MOVEMENT GOAL COMPLETED ◯

WATER _____

WHAT AM I PROUD OF TODAY?

WHEN I MOVED MY BODY, I FELT:

_____
_____
_____

WHAT AM I LOOKING FORWARD TO TOMORROW?

_____
_____
_____

WEEK 3
MOTIVATION

KAYLA'S PEP TALK:
MOTIVATION

Motivation is something we talk about *all the time* here at Sweat. We know push-ups can be hard. Lifting heavier weights requires you to dig deep. And when you see burpees in one of my circuits? Well, I *know* they're not exactly everyone's favourite exercise.

Back in Week 1 of your reboot journey, we talked about how getting in touch with your why can help set you up for success. But how do we get from A to B on your fitness journey on those days when your drive just isn't there?

Before we get into how to stay fired up on your fitness journey, let's take a moment to celebrate how far you've come!

You've already smashed out two weeks of workouts and I bet you're feeling a sense of accomplishment, even if you're feeling a bit achy or some days haven't gone to plan. Celebrate this – you've earned it.

For many of us, one of the hardest things about rebooting our fitness routine isn't finding the motivation to get started. It's unlocking the drive to keep going, *especially* if you don't feel like you're making progress. In my experience, this often occurs halfway through a new program (the honeymoon phase of your fitness journey might have *well* worn off!), which is why motivation is the focus for Week 3.

I want you to know that we've *all* had those moments where we've felt less than inspired by the thought of putting on a sports bra, rolling out the yoga mat and picking up that set of dumbbells. Even when you *know* how good exercise is for you (and just how incredible that post-workout endorphin rush is), it's not unusual for that unfolded pile of washing to suddenly look super appealing right before your session starts.

That's why I like to treat my training time like an important appointment I've made with myself. I wouldn't cancel a work meeting 10 minutes before it was about to begin, and getting into the habit of thinking about my workouts in the same way has helped a lot.

No matter how disciplined you become, it's important to remember that your drive to move will come in waves and there will be times when you're just not feeling it. What's important is what you do in these moments, and this is where I want you to tap into the power of *intrinsic motivation*.

While there are a number of different motivation systems, research suggests that when your motivation comes from within, you're moved to act for the joy or challenge of the activity. This is in contrast to *extrinsic motivation*, which is driven by external pressures or benefits.[2]

For example, you might play basketball with your friends because it's a fun part of your week, not because you're trying to win a championship. Perhaps someone you know paints in their spare time because it's an activity that fills their cup, not because they're hoping to sell their art. When you're intrinsically motivated, it's the *act of doing* that brings you joy – not the results.

I want you to think about what you enjoy most about your workouts *and* how you want to feel – before, during and after each Sweat session. Maybe you want a sense of empowerment and pride. You could be after that feeling of progress that comes when you master something new (hello, push-ups). Perhaps you're chasing that mood-boosting endorphin rush or happy feeling after working out with your friend. Or you might simply want to feel strong, fit and healthy.

Another handy motivation hack to have in your pocket is the five-minute rule. It's a sneaky cognitive behavioural technique that's perfect for those days when your motivation and energy levels are low. The premise is simple. Just set a timer for five minutes, start your session and give it your best. When the timer goes off, reassess how you feel. If the timer goes off and you're still not feeling it, you're done! You'll know that today's just not your day. But as most of us know, once you've made it through the first five minutes, you've passed the biggest hurdle of all: getting started.

Years ago, I had a client who struggled with motivation, and I told her not to think about the workout – just get to the gym and touch the door. By that point, she was already committed, and the rest of the workout was easy.

So, hit play on your most motivating playlist, get dressed, find a workout space that feels good and reconnect with your why. It's time to say yes to you. Let's go.

Let people be
your power.

WEEK 3 KEY: COMMUNITY

One of the most common questions I get asked as a trainer is how to stay motivated. How do you get up and go when you just don't feel like it, when it gets boring, when you're tired, when you've achieved your goals, when you don't have the time or when you're not seeing the progress that you hoped for?

I could give you all the advice you've heard before about setting new goals, keeping it fun, or learning to develop discipline alongside motivation, but something I don't think people talk about enough when it comes to maintaining that sense of drive is the power of people.

When I went from training women in one-on-one to group sessions and eventually running boot camps with thousands of women, I saw just how much of a difference it makes to have other women by your side the entire time – sweating and puffing and encouraging each other.

Every day, I see women in my community coming together online, cheering each other on, sharing their experiences and feeling motivated to continue because they feel so connected and part of something bigger than themselves. And these women motivate me, too. In those moments when I'm lacking motivation, it's *your* Instagram handle I'm looking at to encourage me to get up and move.

Tapping into the power of people and community isn't just limited to being part of a group training session or connecting online. It's about sharing your fitness experience with other people in whatever way feels uplifting and motivating for you.

Even if you love plugging in your headphones and working out on your own, your fitness journey will be a hell of a lot easier if you don't feel like you're in it alone.

This week, I want you to think about what this might look like for *you*. It could be letting your family or friends know what your goals are or how your journey is going so they can offer encouragement (or hold you accountable!). It could be asking a friend or your partner if they want to join you for walks or workouts. It could be following other women online who you find inspiring, and letting *their* energy motivate you.

Although this is something you're doing for you, don't forget that it's also something you can do with others, together.

WEEK 3 MEAL PLANNER

Tip: Have a shopping list handy while you record your plans.

MONDAY

BREAKFAST

SNACK

LUNCH

SNACK

DINNER

TUESDAY

B

S

L

S

D

WEDNESDAY

B

S

L

S

D

THURSDAY

B

S

L

S

D

FRIDAY

B

S

L

S

D

SATURDAY

B

S

L

S

D

SUNDAY

B

S

L

S

D

WEEK 3 MOVEMENT PLAN

WEEKLY GOAL: Complete any 3 sessions
EQUIPMENT: Light dumbbells (2–4 kg)

SESSION 1
WALK

EXERCISE	REPS/TIME
Walk, treadmill or outdoor	30 minutes

SESSION 2
MOBILITY
CIRCUIT

EXERCISE	REPS/TIME	LAPS
Lying thoracic rotation (page 99)	16 reps	2
Floor slides (page 97)	30 seconds	
Quad stretch (page 89)	60 seconds (30 per side)	
Hamstring stretch (page 86)	60 seconds (30 per side)	

SESSION 3
STRENGTH
WORKOUT 1
CIRCUIT

EXERCISE	REPS/TIME	LAPS
Dumbbell goblet squat (page 106)	10 reps	3
Dumbbell curl and press (page 125)	10 reps	
Lateral lunge to knee up (page 141)	20 reps (10 per side)	
Side plank and hip dip (page 136)	20 seconds	
Rest	30 seconds	

SESSION 4
STRENGTH
WORKOUT 2
CIRCUIT

EXERCISE	REPS/TIME	LAPS
Double pulse squat (page 103)	12 reps	3
Glute bridge and opening (page 114)	12 reps	
Lying-down push-up (knees) (page 123)	8 reps	
Single-arm and leg jackknife (page 129)	20 reps	
Rest	30 seconds	

SESSION 5
STRENGTH
WORKOUT 2
CIRCUIT

EXERCISE	REPS/TIME	LAPS
Front lunge (page 109)	20 reps (10 per side)	4
Squat and high reach (page 140)	12 reps	
Split stance hip thrust (chair) (page 119)	12 reps	
Plank and shoulder tap (knees) (page 133)	16 reps	
Rest	30 seconds	

WEEK 3 MOTIVATION

WEEK 3: DAY 1

Date: /   /

HOW AM I FEELING TODAY?

_____

_____

_____

I AM GRATEFUL FOR:

_____

_____

_____

MOVEMENT GOAL:

_____

SOMETHING I WANT TO ACHIEVE TODAY:

_____

_____

_____

EVENING CHECK-IN

MOVEMENT GOAL COMPLETED ◯

WATER _____

WHAT AM I PROUD OF TODAY?

_____

_____

_____

WHEN I MOVED MY BODY, I FELT:

_____

_____

WHAT AM I LOOKING FORWARD TO TOMORROW?

_____

_____

_____

WEEK 3: DAY 2

Date: /   /

HOW AM I FEELING TODAY?

_____

_____

_____

I AM GRATEFUL FOR:

_____

_____

_____

MOVEMENT GOAL:

_____

SOMETHING I WANT TO ACHIEVE TODAY:

_____

_____

EVENING CHECK-IN

MOVEMENT GOAL COMPLETED ◯

WATER _____

WHAT AM I PROUD OF TODAY?

_____

_____

_____

WHEN I MOVED MY BODY, I FELT:

_____

_____

WHAT AM I LOOKING FORWARD TO TOMORROW?

_____

_____

_____

WEEK 3: DAY 3

Date: /   /

HOW AM I FEELING TODAY?

_____

_____

_____

I AM GRATEFUL FOR:

_____

_____

_____

MOVEMENT GOAL:

_____

SOMETHING I WANT TO ACHIEVE TODAY:

_____

_____

EVENING CHECK-IN

MOVEMENT GOAL COMPLETED ◯

WATER _____

WHAT AM I PROUD OF TODAY?

WHEN I MOVED MY BODY, I FELT:

_____

_____

_____

WHAT AM I LOOKING FORWARD TO TOMORROW?

_____

_____

_____

WEEK 3: DAY 4

Date: / /

HOW AM I FEELING TODAY?

_____

_____

_____

I AM GRATEFUL FOR:

_____

_____

_____

MOVEMENT GOAL:

_____

SOMETHING I WANT TO ACHIEVE TODAY:

_____

_____

_____

EVENING CHECK-IN

MOVEMENT GOAL COMPLETED ◯

WATER _____

WHAT AM I PROUD OF TODAY?

WHEN I MOVED MY BODY, I FELT:

_____

_____

_____

_____

WHAT AM I LOOKING FORWARD TO TOMORROW?

_____

_____

_____

You don't have to be great to start, but you have to start to be great.

WEEK 3: DAY 5

HOW AM I FEELING TODAY?

_____
_____
_____

I AM GRATEFUL FOR:

_____
_____
_____

MOVEMENT GOAL:

_____

SOMETHING I WANT TO ACHIEVE TODAY:

_____
_____
_____

EVENING CHECK-IN

MOVEMENT GOAL COMPLETED ◯

WATER _____

WHAT AM I PROUD OF TODAY?

WHEN I MOVED MY BODY, I FELT:

_____   _____
_____   _____
_____   _____

WHAT AM I LOOKING FORWARD TO TOMORROW?

_____
_____
_____

WEEK 3: DAY 6

Date: / /

HOW AM I FEELING TODAY?

_____
_____
_____

I AM GRATEFUL FOR:

_____
_____
_____

MOVEMENT GOAL:

_____

SOMETHING I WANT TO ACHIEVE TODAY:

_____
_____
_____

EVENING CHECK-IN

MOVEMENT GOAL COMPLETED ◯

WATER _____

WHAT AM I PROUD OF TODAY?

_____
_____
_____

WHEN I MOVED MY BODY, I FELT:

_____
_____

WHAT AM I LOOKING FORWARD TO TOMORROW?

_____
_____
_____

WEEK 3: DAY 7

Date: /   /

HOW AM I FEELING TODAY?

_____

_____

_____

I AM GRATEFUL FOR:

_____

_____

_____

MOVEMENT GOAL:

_____

SOMETHING I WANT TO ACHIEVE TODAY:

_____

_____

_____

EVENING CHECK-IN

MOVEMENT GOAL COMPLETED ◯

WATER _____

WHAT AM I PROUD OF TODAY?

WHEN I MOVED MY BODY, I FELT:

_____   _____

_____   _____

_____   _____

WHAT AM I LOOKING FORWARD TO TOMORROW?

_____

_____

_____

WEEK 4
MOMENTUM

KAYLA'S PEP TALK:
MOMENTUM

Welcome to Week 4 of your reboot journey – and congratulations! How good does it feel to be so close to your goal?

Before we get stuck into the last week of our training together (it's safe to say I've saved the best till last!), I want to set you up to keep powering ahead, this week *and* beyond.

After all, momentum isn't just something you want to build for a single workout or month, but something you want to foster long-term, to drive you forward in every aspect of your training and life.

I want momentum to be your focus this week, as we tackle these final workouts and start to look ahead at what's next. Have a think about what's challenged you the most so far *and* what you're loving about your new fitness routine. Write these down so you can come back and look at them later!

Perhaps you've progressed from doing push-ups on your knees to your toes, are loving making nourishing meals from the reboot recipes, have found you've been waking up energised or feel like your mindset is improving. These wins are *all* worth celebrating and are something to remember in those moments when your inner critic starts telling you you're not moving forward.

But what about the things that *haven't* gone to plan? Every now and then we all face setbacks in our fitness journeys (I know I've had my fair share over the years, from endo surgery to getting sick just before a Sweat Challenge!). A setback might hold you back for a single session, an entire week or perhaps even longer – and it's important to know what to do when you encounter one, so you don't lose your momentum for good.

From illness or injury, to a change in schedule, or exercise boredom creeping its way into your routine, setbacks don't necessarily need to derail your progress. Instead, think of them as an opportunity to learn – about yourself, your body and your mindset – so you can come back even stronger.

One of the best things to do to maintain your momentum is to make a plan and find a rhythm. I've said it before and I'll say it again and again: treat your workouts like appointments you've made with yourself.

Struggling to make these me-time appointments or finding you're consistently cancelling on yourself? It's time to get organised. Pack your gym bag the night before. Set up your at-home workout space so it's ready to go when you get back from work. Go to bed earlier if you keep hitting the snooze button instead of making your morning workout. Striving to be the best version of you won't always be easy (and will look different each day), but it's always worth it.

If your routine feels flat, mix it up! Switch up your environment and find other ways to lead an active lifestyle – like cycling to work, enjoying family walks on the weekend or working out at a different time of day. Perhaps your training style just isn't serving you any more and you're ready to try something totally new! If you've already signed up to the Sweat app, take a look at the On Demand tab where you'll find thousands of workouts in a range of different training styles.

If you're finding it hard to overcome a setback, I encourage you to speak up and connect with your support network. Whether it's your partner, parents, siblings, friends or women within the Sweat Community, having a group of people that you *know* are cheering you on can make a world of difference. And those times when you're really struggling to overcome negative self-talk? It's okay not to be okay, and it's always okay to seek out the support of a medical professional if you're struggling with your mental health.

Make sure that you remember there's never a bad time to hit reboot on your goals. While we often think the start of a new year is the best time to start (with Mondays coming in a close second!), you don't need a fresh calendar to start chasing your goals. This book has been designed so you can revisit them again and again, any time of the year, complete with an additional set of journal pages for future reboots.

And don't forget what we discussed at the beginning of this journey – your why. This is your reason to love movement and it's there to help you keep moving or help reignite your fitness fire. Use it to fuel your fitness momentum – this week and beyond.

Fuel yourself
forward.

WEEK 4 KEY: FUEL

What you do when you're *not* exercising is just as important as your training time. That's why it's so important to fuel your body in a positive way. Because when you're not focusing on recharging your batteries and nourishing your body, it can be easy to lose momentum.

While we've included recipes in this book, you might have noticed they are definitely *not* a diet plan. Personally, I don't restrict what I eat. I choose not to cut out certain food groups and instead enjoy a wide range of foods and flavours. Anyone who knows me knows just how much enjoyment I get from eating and sharing a great meal with my family. Maintaining a healthy and balanced diet *without* restriction is what works for me.

However you're fuelling your body, make sure it makes you feel good, that it's healthy and that you enjoy it. And yes, include all of your favourite foods.

I also want to encourage you to nourish your body through good hydration and sleep habits. Drinking enough water is so important if you want to feel your best. Being dehydrated sets you up for a negative loop of brain fog, poor digestion, headaches and fatigue, which can make you want to reach for caffeine or sugary snacks, causing further dehydration and energy slumps. Drink your water!

A solid night of sleep can also influence how you feel physically and mentally. As a mum of two, let me tell you I'm not kidding when I say I truly understand how sleep deprivation is a form of torture! While maintaining good sleeping habits can be tough at times (new mums, I see you), a good night's sleep starts with your daily habits.

Getting 6–8 hours of sleep is a must, and that doesn't mean hours in bed, it means hours spent *asleep*. You might need to make some adjustments to your daytime routine to ensure you can get to sleep (and stay asleep!) at the right time. Regular exercise makes a huge difference, as can spending time outdoors, only napping when you need to, embracing relaxation techniques like mindfulness, taking some time off from technology and avoiding caffeine in the second half of the day.

Above everything, I want your fitness journey to *improve* your energy and your life. Tick that box and you'll have momentum for years to come.

WEEK 4 MEAL PLANNER

Tip: Have a shopping list handy while you record your plans.

MONDAY

BREAKFAST

SNACK

LUNCH

SNACK

DINNER

TUESDAY

B

S

L

S

D

WEDNESDAY

B

S

L

S

D

THURSDAY

B

S

L

S

D

FRIDAY

B

S

L

S

D

SATURDAY

B

S

L

S

D

SUNDAY

B

S

L

S

D

WEEK 4 MOVEMENT PLAN

WEEKLY GOAL: Complete any 3 sessions
EQUIPMENT: Light dumbbells (2–4 kg)

SESSION 1
WALK

EXERCISE	REPS/TIME
Walk, treadmill or outdoor	35 minutes

SESSION 2
MOBILITY
CIRCUIT

EXERCISE	REPS/TIME	LAPS
Hip flexor to hamstring (page 92)	60 seconds	2
Deep squat and rotation (page 91)	40 seconds	
Glute stretch (page 85)	60 seconds (30 per side)	
Butterfly stretch (page 84)	40 seconds	

SESSION 3
STRENGTH
WORKOUT 1
CIRCUIT

EXERCISE	REPS/TIME	LAPS
Dumbbell front squat (page 107)	12 reps	3
Dumbbell bent-over row (page 126)	12 reps	
Reverse lunge and knee (page 112)	24 reps (12 per side)	
High plank and shoulder tap (page 134)	30 seconds	
Ab bike to jackknife (page 130)	24 reps	
Rest	30 seconds	

SESSION 4
STRENGTH
WORKOUT 2
CIRCUIT

EXERCISE	REPS/TIME	LAPS
Double pulse sumo squat (page 104)	15 reps	4
Single-leg glute bridge (page 116)	16 reps	
Tricep dip (chair) (page 124)	10 reps	
Ab bikes (page 128)	24 reps	
Side plank (page 135)	40 seconds (20 per side)	
Rest	30 seconds	

SESSION 5
STRENGTH
WORKOUT 3
CIRCUIT

EXERCISE	REPS/TIME	LAPS
Lateral lunge (page 110)	24 reps (12 per side)	4
Modified walkout burpee (chair) (page 138)	15 reps	
Single-leg hip thrust (chair) (page 120)	16 reps	
Plank (toes) (page 132)	20 seconds	
Standing X crunch (page 137)	20 reps (10 per side)	
Rest	30 seconds	

WEEK 4: DAY 1

Date: / /

HOW AM I FEELING TODAY?

_____

_____

_____

I AM GRATEFUL FOR:

_____

_____

_____

MOVEMENT GOAL:

_____

SOMETHING I WANT TO ACHIEVE TODAY:

_____

_____

_____

EVENING CHECK-IN

MOVEMENT GOAL COMPLETED ◯

WATER _____

WHAT AM I PROUD OF TODAY?

WHEN I MOVED MY BODY, I FELT:

_____

_____

_____

WHAT AM I LOOKING FORWARD TO TOMORROW?

_____

_____

_____

WEEK 4: DAY 2

Date: / /

HOW AM I FEELING TODAY?

_____

_____

_____

I AM GRATEFUL FOR:

_____

_____

_____

MOVEMENT GOAL:

_____

SOMETHING I WANT TO ACHIEVE TODAY:

_____

_____

_____

EVENING CHECK-IN

MOVEMENT GOAL COMPLETED ◯

WATER _____

WHAT AM I PROUD OF TODAY?

WHEN I MOVED MY BODY, I FELT:

_____   _____

_____   _____

_____   _____

WHAT AM I LOOKING FORWARD TO TOMORROW?

_____

_____

_____

WEEK 4: DAY 3

Date: /   /

HOW AM I FEELING TODAY?

I AM GRATEFUL FOR:

MOVEMENT GOAL:

SOMETHING I WANT TO ACHIEVE TODAY:

EVENING CHECK-IN

MOVEMENT GOAL COMPLETED ◯

WATER

WHAT AM I PROUD OF TODAY?

WHEN I MOVED MY BODY, I FELT:

WHAT AM I LOOKING FORWARD TO TOMORROW?

WEEK 4: DAY 4

Date: /   /

HOW AM I FEELING TODAY?

_____

_____

_____

I AM GRATEFUL FOR:

_____

_____

_____

MOVEMENT GOAL:

_____

SOMETHING I WANT TO ACHIEVE TODAY:

_____

_____

_____

EVENING CHECK-IN

MOVEMENT GOAL COMPLETED ◯

WATER _____

WHAT AM I PROUD OF TODAY?

WHEN I MOVED MY BODY, I FELT:

_____   _____

_____   _____

_____   _____

WHAT AM I LOOKING FORWARD TO TOMORROW?

_____

_____

_____

You'll never know your full potential unless you push yourself to find it.

WEEK 4: DAY 5

Date: / /

HOW AM I FEELING TODAY?

_____
_____
_____

I AM GRATEFUL FOR:

_____
_____
_____

MOVEMENT GOAL:

_____

SOMETHING I WANT TO ACHIEVE TODAY:

_____
_____
_____

EVENING CHECK-IN

MOVEMENT GOAL COMPLETED ◯

WATER _____

WHAT AM I PROUD OF TODAY?

WHEN I MOVED MY BODY, I FELT:

_____   _____
_____   _____
_____   _____

WHAT AM I LOOKING FORWARD TO TOMORROW?

_____
_____
_____

WEEK 4: DAY 6

Date: /   /

HOW AM I FEELING TODAY?

_____

_____

_____

I AM GRATEFUL FOR:

_____

_____

_____

MOVEMENT GOAL:

_____

SOMETHING I WANT TO ACHIEVE TODAY:

_____

_____

_____

EVENING CHECK-IN

MOVEMENT GOAL COMPLETED ◯

WATER _____

WHAT AM I PROUD OF TODAY?

WHEN I MOVED MY BODY, I FELT:

_____   _____

_____   _____

_____   _____

WHAT AM I LOOKING FORWARD TO TOMORROW?

_____

_____

_____

WEEK 4: DAY 7

Date: /   /

HOW AM I FEELING TODAY?

_____

_____

_____

I AM GRATEFUL FOR:

_____

_____

_____

MOVEMENT GOAL:

_____

SOMETHING I WANT TO ACHIEVE TODAY:

_____

_____

_____

EVENING CHECK-IN

MOVEMENT GOAL COMPLETED ◯

WATER _____

WHAT AM I PROUD OF TODAY?

WHEN I MOVED MY BODY, I FELT:

_____

_____

_____

_____

WHAT AM I LOOKING FORWARD TO TOMORROW?

_____

_____

_____

WHAT'S NEXT?

YOU'VE GOT THIS

Making your health and fitness a priority is no small feat and you should be *so* proud of yourself for everything you've put into your reboot journey.

Over the last four weeks, I'm sure you've had your fair share of happy, empowered, accomplished moments, alongside those times you may have felt deflated or unmotivated, or even wondered if you had it in you to keep going.

Let me tell you, *you do.*

On social media, we tend to see the shiny, perfect moments – the Sweat program completed from start to finish, lifting heavier dumbbells, the first push-ups you completed on your toes. And while those highs are absolutely worth celebrating, it's so important to recognise that they wouldn't mean as much without the lows.

If getting fit was easy, everyone would already have done it. And as much as regular exercise feels good and benefits your life, there's no denying it also takes grit, effort, patience, determination, resilience and Sweat. And these amazing qualities are what you're building in every single moment when you feel like you're swimming upstream.

Those tougher moments might not feel as good as the wins, but they're worthwhile in another way. The Sweat team and I hope, as you continue onwards with your workouts *and* your life, that your fitness journey teaches you to never shy away from discomfort or say no to a challenge, as it's only going to make you better in the end.

For many people, the end of a health and fitness reboot means looking for visible signs of progress and achievement, whether that's how many workouts you completed, how many steps you clocked up, or how many push-ups you can now do.

We love celebrating these wins at Sweat, but as you come to the end of your reboot, I also want you to reflect on or write down some of those times over the past four weeks when, despite thinking you didn't have it in you, you showed yourself that you did. Because for me, it's *that* practice – of getting up each time you're feeling down – that makes me most proud as your trainer. *That's* going to get you so much further than only focusing on numbers.

Maybe it was the mornings you didn't hit snooze, the Sweat sessions where you went for *one* more rep than you thought was possible, or the days when you couldn't bear to face a structured workout but still ventured outside for a walk and got your body moving.

When I look back on my own experiences with returning to fitness after having children or being unwell, the sense of pride at how far I've come wouldn't exist if I'd never had the tough moments along the way. Seriously. Give yourself some credit.

Rising to each challenge doesn't have to be something you do alone. Community and connection can become your secret weapon and carry you to heights you couldn't reach on your own.

From running one-on-one training sessions and group boot camps to launching a viral program, global events and now being the head trainer at Sweat, I know firsthand how powerful it is to Sweat together. Nothing supercharges a workout like telling each other between each breathless rep to keep going and not give up. In these sessions, the power of community can ignite in a way I didn't even know was possible.

Women are sharing their experiences across social media, forging friendships across streets and borders, and cheerleading for people they've never met. If you feel like you're in this alone at any moment, I can assure you, you're already part of an incredible community of women.

If you're ready to take your fitness journey to the next level or discover what it feels like to be part of something much bigger than yourself, I would love for you to join me on the Sweat app. The Sweat Community is ready to welcome you with open arms.

Not sure where to begin? Start with a free trial and get familiar with the app. Check out the 50+ programs, thousands of workouts, world-class trainers and plenty of education resources, learn how the Community forum works, and get a taste of why thousands of women choose to Sweat.

Want to try the program that started my own crazy journey? Last year I relaunched OG Kayla, the 28-minute program that transformed the fitness journeys of thousands of women around the world. I'm a *little* bit biased, but I reckon you're going to love it.

To make it even easier to keep going, use the QR code opposite or head to **Sweat.com/Reboot** to unlock your exclusive offer. Try a range of the on-demand workouts to see what you like, or give another one of my programs like Low Impact with Kayla a go.

So, four weeks are done and dusted, just like that. Are you ready to see what else is possible?

REBOOT REFLECTIONS

HOW DO I FEEL NOW THAT I'VE COMPLETED MY REBOOT?

_____

_____

_____

WHAT DID I FIND CHALLENGING?

_____

_____

_____

WHEN WERE THE MOMENTS I PROVED TO MYSELF WHAT I'M CAPABLE OF?

_____

_____

_____

WHAT DO I FEEL PROUDEST OF?

_____

_____

_____

WHAT DO I WANT TO TRY NEXT?

_____

_____

_____

NOTES

WEEK 1: DAY 1

Date: /   /

HOW AM I FEELING TODAY?

_____

_____

I AM GRATEFUL FOR:

_____

_____

MOVEMENT GOAL:

_____

SOMETHING I WANT TO ACHIEVE TODAY:

_____

_____

EVENING CHECK-IN

MOVEMENT GOAL COMPLETED ◯

WATER _____

WHAT AM I PROUD OF TODAY?

WHEN I MOVED MY BODY, I FELT:

_____   _____

_____   _____

WHAT AM I LOOKING FORWARD TO TOMORROW?

_____

_____

WEEK 1: DAY 2

Date: / /

HOW AM I FEELING TODAY?

_____

_____

_____

I AM GRATEFUL FOR:

_____

_____

_____

MOVEMENT GOAL:

_____

SOMETHING I WANT TO ACHIEVE TODAY:

_____

_____

_____

EVENING CHECK-IN

MOVEMENT GOAL COMPLETED ◯

WATER _____

WHAT AM I PROUD OF TODAY?

WHEN I MOVED MY BODY, I FELT:

_____   _____

_____   _____

_____   _____

WHAT AM I LOOKING FORWARD TO TOMORROW?

_____

_____

_____

WHAT'S NEXT?

WEEK 1: DAY 3

Date: /   /

HOW AM I FEELING TODAY?

_____

_____

_____

I AM GRATEFUL FOR:

_____

_____

_____

MOVEMENT GOAL:

_____

SOMETHING I WANT TO ACHIEVE TODAY:

_____

_____

_____

EVENING CHECK-IN

MOVEMENT GOAL COMPLETED ◯

WATER _____

WHAT AM I PROUD OF TODAY?

WHEN I MOVED MY BODY, I FELT:

_____   _____

_____   _____

_____   _____

WHAT AM I LOOKING FORWARD TO TOMORROW?

_____

_____

_____

WEEK 1: DAY 4

Date: / /

HOW AM I FEELING TODAY?

_____

_____

_____

I AM GRATEFUL FOR:

_____

_____

_____

MOVEMENT GOAL:

_____

SOMETHING I WANT TO ACHIEVE TODAY:

_____

_____

_____

EVENING CHECK-IN

MOVEMENT GOAL COMPLETED ◯

WATER _____

WHAT AM I PROUD OF TODAY?

WHEN I MOVED MY BODY, I FELT:

_____   _____

_____   _____

_____   _____

WHAT AM I LOOKING FORWARD TO TOMORROW?

_____

_____

_____

WHAT'S NEXT?

When you feel like quitting, think about why you started.

WEEK 1: DAY 5

Date: /   /

HOW AM I FEELING TODAY?

_____

_____

_____

I AM GRATEFUL FOR:

_____

_____

_____

MOVEMENT GOAL:

_____

SOMETHING I WANT TO ACHIEVE TODAY:

_____

_____

_____

EVENING CHECK-IN

MOVEMENT GOAL COMPLETED ◯

WATER _____

WHAT AM I PROUD OF TODAY?

WHEN I MOVED MY BODY, I FELT:

WHAT AM I LOOKING FORWARD TO TOMORROW?

WHAT'S NEXT?

WEEK 1: DAY 6

Date: / /

HOW AM I FEELING TODAY?

_____

_____

_____

I AM GRATEFUL FOR:

_____

_____

_____

MOVEMENT GOAL:

_____

SOMETHING I WANT TO ACHIEVE TODAY:

_____

_____

EVENING CHECK-IN

MOVEMENT GOAL COMPLETED ◯

WATER _____

WHAT AM I PROUD OF TODAY?

WHEN I MOVED MY BODY, I FELT:

_____   _____

_____   _____

_____   _____

WHAT AM I LOOKING FORWARD TO TOMORROW?

_____

_____

_____

WEEK 1: DAY 7

Date: / /

HOW AM I FEELING TODAY?

_____

_____

_____

I AM GRATEFUL FOR:

_____

_____

_____

MOVEMENT GOAL:

_____

SOMETHING I WANT TO ACHIEVE TODAY:

_____

_____

_____

EVENING CHECK-IN

MOVEMENT GOAL COMPLETED ◯

WATER _____

WHAT AM I PROUD OF TODAY?

WHEN I MOVED MY BODY, I FELT:

_____

_____

_____

_____

WHAT AM I LOOKING FORWARD TO TOMORROW?

_____

_____

_____

WHAT'S NEXT?

WEEK 2: DAY 1

Date: / /

HOW AM I FEELING TODAY?

_____

_____

_____

I AM GRATEFUL FOR:

_____

_____

_____

MOVEMENT GOAL:

_____

SOMETHING I WANT TO ACHIEVE TODAY:

_____

_____

_____

EVENING CHECK-IN

MOVEMENT GOAL COMPLETED ◯

WATER _____

WHAT AM I PROUD OF TODAY?

WHEN I MOVED MY BODY, I FELT:

_____

_____

_____

WHAT AM I LOOKING FORWARD TO TOMORROW?

_____

_____

_____

WEEK 2: DAY 2

Date: /   /

HOW AM I FEELING TODAY?

_____
_____
_____

I AM GRATEFUL FOR:

_____
_____
_____

MOVEMENT GOAL:

_____

SOMETHING I WANT TO ACHIEVE TODAY:

_____
_____
_____

EVENING CHECK-IN

MOVEMENT GOAL COMPLETED ◯

WATER _____

WHAT AM I PROUD OF TODAY?

_____
_____
_____

WHEN I MOVED MY BODY, I FELT:

_____
_____
_____

WHAT AM I LOOKING FORWARD TO TOMORROW?

_____
_____
_____

WHAT'S NEXT?

WEEK 2: DAY 3

Date: / /

HOW AM I FEELING TODAY?

_____

_____

_____

I AM GRATEFUL FOR:

_____

_____

_____

MOVEMENT GOAL:

_____

SOMETHING I WANT TO ACHIEVE TODAY:

_____

_____

_____

EVENING CHECK-IN

MOVEMENT GOAL COMPLETED ◯

WATER _____

WHAT AM I PROUD OF TODAY?

WHEN I MOVED MY BODY, I FELT:

_____   _____

_____   _____

_____

WHAT AM I LOOKING FORWARD TO TOMORROW?

_____

_____

_____

WEEK 2: DAY 4

Date: / /

HOW AM I FEELING TODAY?

_____

_____

_____

I AM GRATEFUL FOR:

_____

_____

_____

MOVEMENT GOAL:

_____

SOMETHING I WANT TO ACHIEVE TODAY:

_____

_____

_____

EVENING CHECK-IN

MOVEMENT GOAL COMPLETED ◯

WATER _____

WHAT AM I PROUD OF TODAY?

WHEN I MOVED MY BODY, I FELT:

_____

_____

_____

_____

_____

_____

WHAT AM I LOOKING FORWARD TO TOMORROW?

_____

_____

_____

WHAT'S NEXT?

Don't be
afraid of
being a
beginner.

WEEK 2: DAY 5

Date: / /

HOW AM I FEELING TODAY?

_____
_____
_____

I AM GRATEFUL FOR:

_____
_____
_____

MOVEMENT GOAL:

_____

SOMETHING I WANT TO ACHIEVE TODAY:

_____
_____
_____

EVENING CHECK-IN

MOVEMENT GOAL COMPLETED ◯

WATER _____

WHAT AM I PROUD OF TODAY?

WHEN I MOVED MY BODY, I FELT:

_____
_____
_____

_____
_____
_____

WHAT AM I LOOKING FORWARD TO TOMORROW?

_____
_____
_____

WHAT'S NEXT?

WEEK 2: DAY 6

Date: / /

HOW AM I FEELING TODAY?

_____
_____
_____
_____

I AM GRATEFUL FOR:

_____
_____
_____

MOVEMENT GOAL:

_____

SOMETHING I WANT TO ACHIEVE TODAY:

_____
_____
_____

EVENING CHECK-IN

MOVEMENT GOAL COMPLETED ◯

WATER _____

WHAT AM I PROUD OF TODAY?

WHEN I MOVED MY BODY, I FELT:

_____   _____
_____   _____
_____   _____

WHAT AM I LOOKING FORWARD TO TOMORROW?

_____
_____
_____

WEEK 2: DAY 7

Date: / /

HOW AM I FEELING TODAY?

_____
_____
_____

I AM GRATEFUL FOR:

_____
_____
_____

MOVEMENT GOAL:

_____

SOMETHING I WANT TO ACHIEVE TODAY:

_____
_____
_____

EVENING CHECK-IN

MOVEMENT GOAL COMPLETED ◯

WATER _____

WHAT AM I PROUD OF TODAY?

WHEN I MOVED MY BODY, I FELT:

_____   _____
_____   _____

WHAT AM I LOOKING FORWARD TO TOMORROW?

_____
_____
_____

WHAT'S NEXT?

WEEK 3: DAY 1

Date: / /

HOW AM I FEELING TODAY?

I AM GRATEFUL FOR:

MOVEMENT GOAL:

SOMETHING I WANT TO ACHIEVE TODAY:

EVENING CHECK-IN

MOVEMENT GOAL COMPLETED ◯

WATER ___

WHAT AM I PROUD OF TODAY?

WHEN I MOVED MY BODY, I FELT:

WHAT AM I LOOKING FORWARD TO TOMORROW?

WEEK 3: DAY 2

Date: / /

HOW AM I FEELING TODAY?

_____
_____
_____
_____

I AM GRATEFUL FOR:

_____
_____
_____
_____

MOVEMENT GOAL:

_____

SOMETHING I WANT TO ACHIEVE TODAY:

_____
_____
_____

EVENING CHECK-IN

MOVEMENT GOAL COMPLETED ○

WATER _____

WHAT AM I PROUD OF TODAY?

WHEN I MOVED MY BODY, I FELT:

_____   _____
_____   _____
_____   _____

WHAT AM I LOOKING FORWARD TO TOMORROW?

_____
_____
_____

WHAT'S NEXT?

WEEK 3: DAY 3

Date: / /

HOW AM I FEELING TODAY?

_____
_____
_____

I AM GRATEFUL FOR:

_____
_____
_____

MOVEMENT GOAL:

_____

SOMETHING I WANT TO ACHIEVE TODAY:

_____
_____
_____

EVENING CHECK-IN

MOVEMENT GOAL COMPLETED ◯

WATER _____

WHAT AM I PROUD OF TODAY?

WHEN I MOVED MY BODY, I FELT:

_____
_____

WHAT AM I LOOKING FORWARD TO TOMORROW?

_____
_____
_____

WEEK 3: DAY 4

Date: / /

HOW AM I FEELING TODAY?

_____
_____
_____

I AM GRATEFUL FOR:

_____
_____
_____

MOVEMENT GOAL:

_____

SOMETHING I WANT TO ACHIEVE TODAY:

_____
_____
_____

EVENING CHECK-IN

MOVEMENT GOAL COMPLETED ◯

WATER _____

WHAT AM I PROUD OF TODAY?

_____

_____

WHEN I MOVED MY BODY, I FELT:

_____

_____

WHAT AM I LOOKING FORWARD TO TOMORROW?

_____
_____
_____

WHAT'S NEXT?

Push *yourself,*
because no
one else is
going to do it
for you.

WEEK 3: DAY 5

Date: /   /

HOW AM I FEELING TODAY?

_____
_____
_____

I AM GRATEFUL FOR:

_____
_____
_____

MOVEMENT GOAL:

_____

SOMETHING I WANT TO ACHIEVE TODAY:

_____
_____
_____

EVENING CHECK-IN

MOVEMENT GOAL COMPLETED ◯

WATER _____

WHAT AM I PROUD OF TODAY?

WHEN I MOVED MY BODY, I FELT:

_____ _____
_____ _____
_____ _____

WHAT AM I LOOKING FORWARD TO TOMORROW?

_____
_____
_____

WHAT'S NEXT?

WEEK 3: DAY 6

Date: /   /

HOW AM I FEELING TODAY?

_____

_____

_____

I AM GRATEFUL FOR:

_____

_____

_____

MOVEMENT GOAL:

_____

SOMETHING I WANT TO ACHIEVE TODAY:

_____

_____

_____

EVENING CHECK-IN

MOVEMENT GOAL COMPLETED ◯

WATER _____

WHAT AM I PROUD OF TODAY?

WHEN I MOVED MY BODY, I FELT:

_____   _____

_____   _____

WHAT AM I LOOKING FORWARD TO TOMORROW?

_____

_____

_____

WEEK 3: DAY 7

Date: / /

HOW AM I FEELING TODAY?

_____
_____
_____

I AM GRATEFUL FOR:

_____
_____
_____

MOVEMENT GOAL:

_____

SOMETHING I WANT TO ACHIEVE TODAY:

_____
_____
_____

EVENING CHECK-IN

MOVEMENT GOAL COMPLETED ◯

WATER _____

WHAT AM I PROUD OF TODAY?

WHEN I MOVED MY BODY, I FELT:

_____   _____
_____   _____
_____   _____

WHAT AM I LOOKING FORWARD TO TOMORROW?

_____
_____
_____

WHAT'S NEXT?

WEEK 4: DAY 1

Date: / /

HOW AM I FEELING TODAY?

_____
_____
_____

I AM GRATEFUL FOR:

_____
_____
_____

MOVEMENT GOAL:

_____

SOMETHING I WANT TO ACHIEVE TODAY:

_____
_____

EVENING CHECK-IN

MOVEMENT GOAL COMPLETED ◯

WATER _____

WHAT AM I PROUD OF TODAY?

WHEN I MOVED MY BODY, I FELT:

_____   _____
_____   _____
_____   _____

WHAT AM I LOOKING FORWARD TO TOMORROW?

_____
_____
_____

WEEK 4: DAY 2

Date: /   /

HOW AM I FEELING TODAY?

_____
_____
_____

I AM GRATEFUL FOR:

_____
_____
_____

MOVEMENT GOAL:

_____

SOMETHING I WANT TO ACHIEVE TODAY:

_____
_____
_____

EVENING CHECK-IN

MOVEMENT GOAL COMPLETED ○

WATER _____

WHAT AM I PROUD OF TODAY?

WHEN I MOVED MY BODY, I FELT:

WHAT AM I LOOKING FORWARD TO TOMORROW?

WHAT'S NEXT?

WEEK 4: DAY 3

Date: ___ / ___ / ___

HOW AM I FEELING TODAY?

_____

_____

_____

I AM GRATEFUL FOR:

_____

_____

_____

MOVEMENT GOAL:

_____

SOMETHING I WANT TO ACHIEVE TODAY:

_____

_____

EVENING CHECK-IN

MOVEMENT GOAL COMPLETED ◯

WATER _____

WHAT AM I PROUD OF TODAY?

WHEN I MOVED MY BODY, I FELT:

_____

_____

WHAT AM I LOOKING FORWARD TO TOMORROW?

_____

_____

_____

WEEK 4: DAY 4

Date: / /

HOW AM I FEELING TODAY?

_____
_____
_____
_____

I AM GRATEFUL FOR:

_____
_____
_____

MOVEMENT GOAL:

_____

SOMETHING I WANT TO ACHIEVE TODAY:

_____
_____

EVENING CHECK-IN

MOVEMENT GOAL COMPLETED ◯

WATER _____

WHAT AM I PROUD OF TODAY?

WHEN I MOVED MY BODY, I FELT:

_____   _____
_____   _____
_____   _____

WHAT AM I LOOKING FORWARD TO TOMORROW?

_____
_____
_____

WHAT'S NEXT?

Today
is the
tomorrow
you talked
about
yesterday.

WEEK 4: DAY 5

Date: /   /

HOW AM I FEELING TODAY?

_____

_____

_____

I AM GRATEFUL FOR:

_____

_____

_____

MOVEMENT GOAL:

_____

SOMETHING I WANT TO ACHIEVE TODAY:

_____

_____

_____

EVENING CHECK-IN

MOVEMENT GOAL COMPLETED ◯

WATER _____

WHAT AM I PROUD OF TODAY?

_____

_____

_____

WHEN I MOVED MY BODY, I FELT:

_____

_____

_____

WHAT AM I LOOKING FORWARD TO TOMORROW?

_____

_____

_____

WHAT'S NEXT?

WEEK 4: DAY 6

Date: / /

HOW AM I FEELING TODAY?

I AM GRATEFUL FOR:

MOVEMENT GOAL:

SOMETHING I WANT TO ACHIEVE TODAY:

EVENING CHECK-IN

MOVEMENT GOAL COMPLETED ◯

WATER _____

WHAT AM I PROUD OF TODAY?

WHEN I MOVED MY BODY, I FELT:

WHAT AM I LOOKING FORWARD TO TOMORROW?

WEEK 4: DAY 7

Date: /   /

HOW AM I FEELING TODAY?

_____

_____

I AM GRATEFUL FOR:

_____

_____

_____

MOVEMENT GOAL:

_____

SOMETHING I WANT TO ACHIEVE TODAY:

_____

_____

EVENING CHECK-IN

MOVEMENT GOAL COMPLETED ◯

WATER _____

WHAT AM I PROUD OF TODAY?

WHEN I MOVED MY BODY, I FELT:

_____   _____

_____   _____

_____

WHAT AM I LOOKING FORWARD TO TOMORROW?

_____

_____

_____

WHAT'S NEXT?

INDEX

RECIPE INDEX

THANKS

At the end of the day, this book would not exist without YOU. I've been asked a few times what I would do if I wasn't in the public eye, and the answer is simple. I'd be a personal trainer. I love my job and it's thanks to you and every single woman in my community who has trained with me that I get to do what I do. Whether you trained with me in my parents' backyard, you came to a boot camp, had the OG BBG PDF, are part of the Sweat Community or started working out with me four weeks ago when you picked up this book – I think you're all incredible.

You might have seen that this book is dedicated to an amazing woman called Deb, who we lost in 2022. Deb, known as @fitwithsweat to her almost 8000 followers, was an OG member who had been with me from the very beginning. Throughout her life, Deb faced more health challenges than any of us should ever have to go through. Her fitness journey actually began under supervision while she was in hospital in 2015, at the direction of her doctor. She then turned to Sweat after being frustrated and upset with how weak she felt and never looked back.

In many ways, Deb was the heart and soul of the Sweat Community. She made so many lifelong friends, built her strength and confidence, found so much joy in her training and celebrated EVERY milestone. I was so lucky to call Deb my friend, and she is still a huge source of motivation and inspiration for me. I miss her every day and this book would not have been possible without her.

To everyone at Sweat who helped transform this book from an idea to the finished copy you have in your hands today – in particular, Alice Brown, Amy Cooper, Anthony Ruggiero, Chelsea Paddick, Dee Riddell, Erin Fisher, Enza Demicoli, Eva Cameron, Liz Rover, Sara Bergstrom and Sydney Wennerstrom – thank you so much for your help and support.

To the team at Penguin Random House who helped bring this book to life, especially Holly Toohey, Izzy Yates and designer Andy Warren, thank you.

And finally, to my incredible family – Jae, Arna, Jax, Mum, Dad, Leah, Mitch, Gigi, Yiayia and Papou and my amazing friends. They say it takes a village, and there's no village I would rather be part of than ours.

Ebury Press, an imprint of Ebury Publishing
20 Vauxhall Bridge Road
London SW1V 2SA

Ebury Press is part of the Penguin Random House group of companies whose addresses can
be found at global.penguinrandomhouse.com

First published in the United Kingdom by Ebury Press in 2024
First published in Australia by Penguin Life in 2024

www.penguin.co.uk

A CIP catalogue record for this book is available from the British Library

The information contained in this book is provided for general purposes only.
It is not intended for and should not be relied upon as medical advice. The publisher
and author are not responsible for any specific health or allergy needs that may require
medical supervision. If you have underlying health problems, intend to change your
diet or lifestyle, or have any doubts about the advice provided in this book, you should
seek the advice of a qualified medical, dietary or other appropriate professional.

Cover design, internal design and typesetting
by Andy Warren Design © Penguin Random House Australia Pty Ltd
Lifestyle and exercise photography by Josh Geelen in collaboration with Sweat
Food photography by William Meppem © Penguin Random House Australia Pty Ltd
Food styling by Lucy Tweed

References:
1. 'Walking: Trim your waistline, improve your health', Mayo Clinic.
2. P. Oudeyer and F. Kaplan (2007), 'What is intrinsic motivation? A typology of computational
approaches', Frontiers Neurorobotics, vol 1 – 2007.

ISBN 9781529932751

Printed and bound in Turkey by Elma Basim

The authorised representative in the EEA is Penguin Random House Ireland, Morrison
Chambers, 32 Nassau Street, Dublin D02 YH68.

Sweat is a leading women's fitness app and global community that's transformed the lives of millions of women around the world. Co-founder and head trainer **Kayla Itsines** has made it her mission to provide women with the tools they need to improve their health and fitness, revolutionising the female fitness landscape and making movement more accessible to women across the globe. Home to over 50 unique programs and more than 13,000 workouts designed by women, for women, Sweat is available in over 145 countries and in eight languages.